Experiencing the Depths of the Holy Spirit:
A Deeper Understanding of the Godhead

By

Prophetess Mary J. Ogenaarekhua

Endorsement

"*Experiencing the Depths of the Holy Spirit* by Prophetess Mary O. is a testimony that the Lord **Holy Spirit** Himself wants us to know Him and to experience Him in a greater measure. The Lord said in Amos 3:7 that He reveals **His secrets** unto **His** servants the prophets. Therefore, you will find glorious secrets about the **Holy Spirit** as He reveals Himself to you in your awesome journey through the chapters of this book. I encourage you to read this book because, 'It is the glory of God to conceal a thing: but the honour of kings is to search out a matter -**Proverbs 25:2**.'"

–Lynne Garbinsky, Chief Operations Officer, THGP/MJM, Atlanta, Georgia.

Dedication

I dedicate this book to **God the Holy Spirit, God the Father** and **God the Son**. **Lord Holy Spirit**, You gave me the words to write in this book and I thank You for also giving me the grace to do it. Lord, concerning this book, You have done through me as it is written in **Psalm 68:11**:

> *"The Lord gave the word: great was the company of those that published it."*

Thanks **Lord Holy Spirit** for teaching me how to hear Your voice for myself and for making me a vessel that You use to teach others how to hear Your voice for themselves as well. It is a great honor to have You as my Teacher. May this book bring You much glory in the name of the Lord Jesus.

I also dedicate this book to all those who seek the truth about God the **Holy Spirit**.

Experiencing the Depths of the Holy Spirit: A Deeper Understanding of the Godhead

Unless otherwise indicated, all scriptures are quoted from the King James and the New International Versions of the Bible.

Published by: **To His Glory Publishing Company, Inc.**
463 Dogwood Drive, NW
Lilburn, GA 30047
(770) 458-7947
www.tohisglorypublishing.com

This Book is available at:
Amazon.com, BarnesandNoble.com, Booksamillion.com, UK, EU, Canada, Australia, etc.

Also, see the **Order Form** at the back of this book or call/ email below to order this book.

(770) 458-7947
www.tohisglorypublishing.com
Email: tohisglorypublishing@yahoo.com

ISBN: 978-0-9854992-2-8

Table of Contents

Preface

This book is the third in a series of three books titled: *Experiencing the Depths of God the Father, Experiencing the Depths of Jesus Christ, and Experiencing the Depths of the Holy Spirit.* I wrote them to help people gain a deeper knowledge of the **Godhead**; also known as the **Trinity**.

My belief is that if you are totally devoted to being led by the **Holy Spirit**, then you owe it to yourself to know Him in depth as you walk with Him. **Since I already wrote about God the Father and the Lord Jesus, this book is devoted solely to the Holy Spirit because I believe that He is the least understood member of the Godhead by Christians.** There are revelations in this book that will help you to know and to draw closer to the **Holy Spirit**.

My desire is that after you have read this book, you will know the **Lord Holy Spirit** in a much deeper and more intimate way than most people can ever dream of. Therefore, if you are serious about knowing Him, this book is for you and may He bless you as you read it.

— Dr. Mary J. Ogenaarekhua

Acknowledgements

Thank You **Lord Holy Spirit** for being my **Teacher** and for helping me to rise up and write what You showed me about Yourself as a member of the **Godhead**. Thanks for Your grace and for Your patience with me in the times when I was slow to get what You were saying to me.

I also want to thank all those who encouraged me to continue to teach and to write what God has taught me no matter what. You have all been a source of great encouragement to me.

Again, thank you Lynne Garbinsky for the many hours that you spent in formatting and laying out this book. You are a steadfast soldier and may the Lord bless you beyond your imagination.

Chapter 1
Our Introduction to the Holy Spirit

Who is the Holy Spirit?

The Hebrew word רוּחַ (ruwach) which is pronounced **roo'-akh** is used to refer to the **Holy Spirit**. It literally means the **wind** or **breath**. The Greek word πνεῦμα (pneuma) which is pronounced **pnyoo'-mah** is also used in reference to **breath** or **breeze** when talking about the **Holy Spirit**. As a result, many people think of the **Holy Spirit** as **wind, breeze,** or **breath**.

The Bible tells us that the **Holy Spirit** is a **divine being** with **a mind, emotion,** and a **will.** He is the creative FORCE and POWER of the Living God. For example, when the Lord Jesus was in the grave after His death, **the Holy Spirit went down into the grave to bring Him back to life.** In other words, when the Lord Jesus died, **God the Father** in heaven sent **His Spirit** into the grave and into hell to raise Him back to life. God works by the POWER of His own Spirit — the **Holy Spirit**! The **Holy Spirit** is also called the **Holy Ghost** or the **Spirit of God.**

All the chapters in this book are meant to reveal the **Holy Spirit** to you in ways that you have never known or understood before. Let us look at the first time we saw the **Holy Spirit** in scriptures.

The Holy Spirit as Part of the Godhead

We were first introduced to the **Holy Spirit** as part of the **Triune God** in the book of **Genesis.** There are many things that are written in scriptures which without the help of the **Holy Spirit,** we cannot even begin to have a clue as to their true and accurate meaning. For example, the Bible talks about more than one person in one God in **Genesis 1:1-3:**

> "In the beginning **God** created the heaven and the earth. 2 And the earth was without form,

and void; and darkness was upon the face of the deep. And **the <u>Spirit of God</u> moved upon the face of the waters.** 3 And **<u>God said</u>,** Let there be light: and there was light."

When you look at the above scripture, you will immediately see **God the Father** in *verse 1,* the **Holy Spirit** in *verse 2,* and **the Word** (the Lord Jesus) in *verse 3.* The reason that we see Him in *verse 2* is because **He is one that activates the Word of God. When God the Father spoke the Word** *(Jesus),* **His Spirit; the Holy Spirit went into action to produce what the Father said.** We again see the **Holy Spirit** in **Genesis 1:26:**

> "And **God said, Let <u>us</u> make man in <u>our</u> image, after our likeness:** and let them have dominion over the fish of the sea, and over the fowl of the air, and over the cattle, and over all the earth, and over every creeping thing that creepeth upon the earth."

Due to my ignorance about the nature of the **Godhead,** when I first read the above scripture, my immediate question was; who was **God** talking to? Who is the <u>us</u> and the <u>our</u> that **God** was referring to? When we have these types of questions or are in need of understanding spiritual truths, it is the **Holy Spirit** that will open our spiritual eyes and give us the understanding that we need. Therefore, we need to really get to know who the **Holy Spirit** is so that He can guide us through scriptures; but before discussing the Person of the **Holy Spirit** in depth, we need to first have a <u>good understanding of the **Godhead** or the **Trinity**.</u> **We need to be well grounded on how the Holy Spirit fits into it.**

The **Godhead** is not a myth and it is not something that a segment of Christians or churches made up. **It is real and the Lord Jesus Himself confirmed the existence of the Godhead or the Trinity during many of His teaching sessions.** He often made references to **God the**

Father, Himself and the **Lord Holy Spirit**. Even His last commandment to the disciples in **Matthew 8:18-20** was an affirmation of the existence of the **Godhead:**

> "And Jesus came and spake unto them, saying, All power is given unto me in heaven and in earth. 19 Go ye therefore, and teach all nations, **baptizing them** in the **name** of **the Father, and of the Son**, and of **the Holy Ghost:** 20 Teaching them to observe all things whatsoever I have commanded you: and, lo, I am with you always, even unto the end of the world."

He promised to send us the **Holy Spirit** while He was here and He did. After His death, resurrection and ascension into heaven, He gave instructions to His Apostles through the **Holy Spirit** as recorded by Luke in **Acts 1:1-3:**

> "…Of all that Jesus began both to do and teach, 2 Until the day in which he was taken up, **after that he through the Holy Ghost had given commandments unto the apostles whom he had chosen:** 3 To whom also **he shewed himself alive after his passion by many infallible proofs, being seen of them forty days**, and speaking of the things pertaining to the kingdom of God."

It was the **Holy Spirit** that took messages from the **Lord Jesus** in heaven and passed them on to the Apostles here on earth. **He is now our only means of communication with both God the Father and the Lord Jesus** *(the Word)***.** This is why the Lord Jesus said of Him in **John 16:14-15** thus:

> "**…For he shall receive of mine, and shall shew it unto you.** 15 All things that the Father hath are mine: therefore said I, that **he shall take of mine, and shall shew it unto you.**"

The Nature of the Godhead or the Trinity

Our basic Christian belief is that there is only **One** God, but this **One God** as we have just read has a **Spirit** (the **Holy Spirit**) and He speaks **the Word** (Jesus Christ). Therefore, when you set out to understand Him, you must know Him as **God the Father**; you must know Him by **His Word** that "became flesh" (Jesus) and you must know Him by **His own Spirit; the Holy Spirit**. This is because the **Father, His Word** (Jesus) and the **Holy Spirit** are the **Three Personalities** that we refer to as the **Godhead** or the **Trinity** and as you can see, He is still just **One God**!

What this means is that Our God is a **Triune God** (consisting of Three Persons) and **the Holy Spirit** is the **Third Person** that makes up the **Godhead** or the **Trinity** (Father, Son and the **Holy Spirit**). We saw the **Godhead** or the **Trinity** right there in **Genesis 1:1-3** as **God the Father** spoke **the Word** (the Lord Jesus) and **His Spirit** (the Holy Spirit) went forth and did what **God the Father** said – *"Let there be light and there was light..."*

We also read in the scriptures that it was the **Holy Spirit** who <u>thawed out</u> the frozen deep (the earth) before **God the Father** began to speak and that it was again the **Holy Spirit** that activated **God the Father's Words** so that what He commanded could become a reality. **Therefore, at any given time since God's dealings with humanity (beginning with Adam), it takes the Father, the Word and the Holy Spirit to make something happen on earth with or for man.**

A lot of unbelievers or non-Christians stumble when it comes to the **Judeo-Christian God** existing in the Three Personalities of **Father, Son** and **Holy Spirit** while still remaining **One God**. The reason that they stumble is because it takes the **Holy Spirit** opening one's eyes to see that throughout scriptures, we are dealing with these Three Personalities that make up the **Godhead. The Godhead is <u>a mystery</u> and God purposely made it so but, He will tell you**

about Himself, about His Word and about His Spirit as He sees you having a genuine desire to know Him better.

Therefore, as born again Christians, we have to thoroughly understand the FORMS in which our God (the Godhead) exist so that we can explain it to those who think that it is a strange concept for God to exist in Three Distinct Persons or Personalities. You need to be able to explain to them that God made man just like Himself — in three parts! Man is a **spirit** (the breath of God in man) having a **soul** (faculties of thought, action, and emotion) and living in a **body**. Just as He made us, God Himself also exists in Three Parts; He has a **Spirit** and a **Soul** and **His Words** have the ability to produce whatever He says by the POWER of His **Holy Spirit**. For example, concerning the Lord Jesus (the Word), **God the Father** gave **His Word** a human body by the POWER of **His Spirit**!

Those who challenge the belief of God's existence in Three Personalities fail to understand the power of the **Almighty God**. They do not know that as the Almighty, God can send both **His Word** and **His Spirit** to wherever He wants and to accomplish whatever He wants accomplished. In other words, God can send **His Spirit** (Holy Spirit) to everyplace on earth; even at the same time if need be. In **Joel 2:28-30**, He promised to pour out **His Spirit** upon all flesh:

> "And it shall come to pass afterward, **that I will pour out my spirit upon all flesh; and your sons and your daughters shall prophesy, your old men shall dream dreams, your young men shall see visions:**
>
> 29 **And also upon the servants and upon the handmaids in those days will I pour out my spirit.** 30 And I will shew wonders in the heavens and in the earth, blood, and fire, and pillars of smoke."

This is one of the reasons why He is God and we are not; **He operates in the earth realm by His Spirit while He Himself is sitting on His throne in Heaven.** For instance, there are people that may never see me; all they will ever hear is my voice or my words as they listen to my CD or read a book that I wrote. Yet, they cannot separate me from my voice (words) on those CDs and from my words in my books. The reason is because **as God Himself explained it to me, a person and his or her words are the same; they are inseparable.**

This knowledge concerning God, His Word and His Spirit should help us to understand that the **Godhead** is not divided and that as matter of fact, they are in unity and they function in unison because it is still the one and same God. **It is not complicated at all for God to function using His own Word** (Jesus) **and His own Spirit.** When you are privileged to see the three of them together in counsel, you will see that although only one voice comes forth, all three of them are actually saying the same thing to you! It is one of the most amazing sights that I have ever seen; the three of them speaking with the same exact voice at the same time! It was truly awesome.

My Vision of the Godhead

I was in a church service one day and the devil decided to scare me by distorting the face of someone sitting near me. He made the person's face to elongate and his ears to enlarge. As the person's ears began to expand and contract, I decided that I was going to defy what I was seeing and instead confess the Word of God in **2 Corinthians 5:7** that says, *"We walk by faith and not by sight."* As I continued to make the confession, God opened heaven to me and I saw a vision of the **Godhead.** Below is an excerpt of my narration of it in the first of these three book series titled; *Experiencing the Depths of God the Father;* pages 109-110:

> *"In this vision, I ran to them (the Father, the Son and the Holy Spirit) in tears crying but when I opened my mouth*

*to launch my complaint about what the devil was doing to me, I heard <u>a voice</u> saying, '**Do not even mention his name for I will show him how much he must suffer for what he has done to my children.**' I stood perplexed before them as the words were being spoken to me because all three of them **seemed** to be speaking and I could not pin-point which one of them was actually the one speaking. I became determined to discover who was speaking among the three of them.*

*It was one of the most hilarious spiritual experiences that I have had because, **God the Father**, **God the Son** and **God the Holy Spirit** were all trying not to burst into laughter as they watched me seriously determine to find out who was speaking among them by checking out each of their mouths as I was hearing the voice! It was some years later that the Lord reminded me of the encounter and how they thought it so funny that I was determined to solve the mystery of the **Godhead**.*

*Due to the ignorance I displayed in the vision above concerning the **Godhead**, you can now understand why the Lord had to teach me about who He is and about the **Godhead**. As a result of the spiritual discernment gifts that He has now given me, I frequently see God the Father and the Lord Jesus in visions and dreams individually and sometimes together. I sometimes see **God the Holy Spirit** by Himself also, but once I saw **God the Father** and **God the Holy Spirit** together in a night vision. Below is the account of my encounter with both **God the Father** and **God the Holy Spirit**. Remember that I am only able to see visions by the <u>aid</u> of the **Holy Spirit** because I am in Christ and **Christ is in God and He is God's Word**. Therefore, all three of the Persons of the **Godhead** are always involved in an activity."*

For a detailed discussion of this second encounter, see the book that I referenced above. As you have seen, although there are Three Personalities in the **Godhead** that make up

Our God, it is the Person of the **Holy Spirit** that uses God's Word to produce whatever **God the Father** and **God the Son** command because both the **Father** and the **Son** are one with the Person of the **Holy Spirit**. **As a matter of fact, the Holy Spirit is the Spirit of the Father and the Son!** This is why He is also called the **"Spirit of Christ"** in **Romans 8:9** and **1 Peter 1:11.** Therefore, as we examine the Person of the **Holy Spirit**, we are not talking of a different God or some independent entity from the **Living God**. I have had other visions and dreams of the **Lord Holy Spirit** by Himself and with **God the Father**. Below is one that I hope will help you to understand both of them better.

I saw the **Holy Spirit** again in the following vision. My first vision of the **Holy Spirit** by Himself was before my vision of the **Godhead** that I just shared with you. It happened in a dream or night vision that I narrated in one of my books titled; *Unveiling the God-mother*; page 53:

"In this dream, I was with my sister who lives in London, England but the scene in the dream quickly changed. It seemed as though I had died and therefore needed to go away beyond the land of the living. My sister decided to escort me on this journey and as we went, we came to a place that marked the division between the land of the living and the dead. My sister could not go with me beyond this point that seemed to separate the land of the living from the land of the dead. I had to make the rest of the journey on my own. I proceeded to go alone, leaving my sister behind.

*Not too long into the journey, **a man dressed in a long white robe** (I did not recognize Him as the **Holy Spirit** then) appeared with a broad smile on His face. He was so humble and so gentle that I stood amazed at Him. He noticed the fear on my face as He stopped to speak with me with a broad smile on His face. He told me not to be afraid, saying, **"This is where you come to receive your assignment and your assignment is to teach those children,"** and*

He pointed to a Roman Catholic Church building where some children seemed to have been locked up in an upstairs classroom. I could hear the noise of the children as He spoke and I wondered who had locked them up in the classroom. As gently and as quickly as He appeared, He left."

It was when I saw the **Holy Spirit** again in my vision of the **Godhead** that I realized that He was the **Holy Spirit**. I shared the above excerpt from one of my previous books with you because I believe that it is relevant to my discussion of the **Lord Holy Spirit** here. I hope that it will help you to see that He is very much a person and that He is not an abstract figure.

He Can Receive Worship

The **Holy Spirit** is God so you can **worship Him** and you can call Him **Lord** and **God**. **As the third Person in the Godhead, He is worthy of our worship and utmost respect. An important fact about the Holy Spirit is that He does not draw attention to Himself.** Instead, He points us to **the Lord Jesus** because of our critical need to be saved or born again and to be led by Him. God gives us eternal life and all other things through His Son, Jesus Christ; therefore, the **Holy Spirit** will not do anything to detract from the works of Christ. He leads us to Christ so that we can choose life — eternal life!

The Lord Holy Spirit is mostly silent about Himself but very vocal about the Lord Jesus. The Lord Jesus told us about this nature of the **Holy Spirit** in **John 16:13-14;** that when the **Holy Spirit** shall come, He will not speak of Himself but will testify about Him:

> "Howbeit when he, the **Spirit of truth**, is come, he will guide you into all truth: **for he shall not speak of himself; but whatsoever he shall hear, that shall he speak:** and he will shew you things to come. *14* **He shall glorify me.**"

He is here to help us become faithful and able witnesses of the Lord Jesus but just because the Holy Spirit does not draw attention to Himself does not mean that we are not to get to know Him or to give Him the worship, honor, adoration and reverence that are due Him. Never forget that He is a part of **God the Father** and so, we must relate to Him as such. **He is always with us and** He is a part of us or to be more concise, we became a part of Him when we were baptized into Christ. As a result, **we can have a personal relationship with Him as our Lord and our God.**

He is the Spirit of Truth

The **Lord Holy Spirit** is the Spirit of Truth and the Lord Jesus said that you shall know the truth and <u>the truth shall make you free</u>. The age old question is: What is truth? The Bible tells us in **John 17:17** that God's Word is truth.

> "Sanctify them through <u>thy truth</u>: **thy word is truth.**"

It is the Lord **Holy Spirit** that helps us understand the Word of God as the only truth that there is. It is our life and it is the cure for ignorance hence the Lord went from village to village, preaching and teaching the people because He knew that the Word of God is the cure for unbelief. The Word of God is also our weapon against the wiles of the devil. For example, the devil is not afraid of anyone who does not know the Word of God or who does not use the Word of God against him. The reason is because the Word of God is the only weapon that destroys the devil's works and breaks his hold over our lives. We learn about the power of the Word of God in **Hebrews 4:12** –it is quick and powerful:

> "**For the word of God is quick, and powerful, and sharper than any two edged sword, piercing even to the dividing asunder of soul and spirit,** and of the joints and marrow, and is a discerner of the thoughts and intents of the heart."

Chapter 2
The Holy Spirit is the Part of the Godhead that Changes Form

God the Father Does Not Change

God the Father is forever constant and He does not change. He declared the following about Himself in **Malachi 3:6:**

> **"For I am the LORD, I change not;** therefore ye sons of Jacob are not consumed."

One of the most notable qualities of **God the Father** is that He cannot alter His Word or lie; He is very faithful to fulfill His promises. Because **God the Father** never changes, the **Holy Spirit** can become many things in order to accomplish whatever **God the Father wants** or desires to accomplish. As a result, you can see Him as **a Person** and He talks to you and He can **flow as oil;** He can **multiply Himself** as the **anointing** on a lot of people at the same time and He can be in the form of a **wind.**

What the scripture above tells us is that God the Father is constant in His form or state of being but through His Spirit; the **Holy Spirit**, He can be in many different forms. This is why we can safely say that the **Holy Spirit** is the part of the **Godhead** that can change forms. Therefore, in order to keep His Word and be all that we want Him to be, He makes use of the **Holy Spirit**. Because of the versatility of the **Holy Spirit**, **God the Father** can be in His Son Jesus, in us the believers and in the earth while He himself does not have to leave heaven.

As a result of this versatility of the **Holy Spirit**, we can safely say that **God the Father's** ability to change **man** or **matter** (material substance); either to restore or to destroy is through the work of the **Holy Spirit**. For instance, the Bible tells us in **Jeremiah 17:9-10** that the heart of man is desperately wicked. To help man and to restore man to Himself, God searches man's heart with **His Spirit** in order to deal with man's wickedness and ungodliness:

> "**The heart is deceitful above all things, and desperately wicked**: who can know it? *10* I the LORD search the heart, I try the reins, even to give every man according to his ways, and according to the fruit of his doings."

Also, God uses His **Holy Spirit** to show us the wickedness in our hearts and He sends the **Holy Spirit** to woo us so that we are willing to forsake our wicked ways. For instance, **the Bible tells us that the carnal mind is in 'enmity' with God and that it is not subject to God's Word.** What this means according to **Romans 8:6-8** is that man is an enemy of God in his mind because he does not want to subject himself to God's Word:

> "For to be carnally minded is death; but to be spiritually minded is life and peace. *7* **Because the carnal mind is enmity against God: for it is not subject to the law of God, neither indeed can be.** *8* So then they that are in the flesh cannot please God."

The truth of this scripture above is evident in our society and in most countries today because many people are now privately and publicly 'right' and 'free' in their own eyes to pursue the things (sins) that God calls abominations and damnable. They cast the Word of God behind them as superstition and they call those who choose to live by God's Word bigots and a bunch of intolerants!

To help restore man and keep man from eternal damnation, God uses the power of the **Holy Spirit** to renew man's mind with His Word in the Bible. The only way man can see his wickedness for what it is and the finished works of Christ (the Word of God) as being life-giving is by the working of the **Holy Spirit**. This is why we are told in **Ephesians 4:20-24:**

> "But ye have not so <u>learned Christ</u>; *21* If so be that ye have heard him, and have been taught by him, <u>as the truth is in Jesus</u>: *22* <u>That ye put off concerning the former conversation the old man, which is corrupt according to the deceitful lusts</u>; *23* **And be renewed in the spirit of your mind**; *24* And that ye put on the new man, which after God is created in righteousness and true holiness."

It takes God using the power of His own **Spirit** and His Word to renew the heart of man before man can walk in love or live a life of godliness. On the other hand, when God wants to bring about His judgment on **man** according to His own Word, He can send hail and thunder storms, lightnings, earthquakes, famines, draughts, pestilences and plagues by the power of the **Holy Spirit**. God restores those who are willing to follow Him and to live by His Word and He can destroy those who insist on rebelling against Him and who are teaching others to do the same. This is why all rebels will be sent to hell.

As for **matter** or <u>material substance</u>, God uses the **Holy Spirit** to <u>alter</u> or change the state of **matter**. For example, He created the heavens and the earth (matter) by sending His **Holy Spirit** to activate **His Word** to bring light out of darkness; land out of the <u>oceans</u> and <u>seas</u>; and the sun, the moon and the stars out of nowhere! He is God. Now, let us look at some of the different forms of the **Holy Spirit**.

Forms of the Holy Spirit

As I said, the Lord Holy Spirit can manifest Himself in the following forms:

- Breath
- Wind
- Oil
- Fire
- Water
- Inspiration

We will examine <u>some of them</u> individually in the following subtitles because they reveal to us the different ways that the **Holy Spirit** manifests Himself and operates on earth today.

The Holy Spirit as the Breath of God

In Christendom, we refer to the **Holy Spirit** as **breath** — **the Breath of God** or **the breath of life**. A good example of the **Holy Spirit** as the breath of God is found in **Genesis 2:7** at the creation of Adam:

> "And the LORD God formed man of the dust of the ground, **and <u>breathed</u> into his nostrils the breath of life** *(His Spirit)*; <u>and man became a living soul</u>."

Without **God's breath** in Adam, man would be as any other creature on earth that God made, but <u>by breathing **His own Spirit** into Adam, God invested Himself in man in a way that He had never done before with His other creations.</u> **This breath made man a part of God and therefore very unique.** This oneness with God was manifested in the judgment that God pronounced on Adam when Adam sinned against God in **Genesis 3:17-19.** I wrote about it in the first of these three books series titled, *Experiencing the Depths of God the Father,* *pages 134-135:*

> *"An Analysis of the Judgments*
> *God in His righteous judgment abased the serpent, re-subjected Eve back under Adam's authority and then judged the ground for Adam's sake... **As for Adam, God***

> *could not bring a curse or a judgment directly upon*
> *Adam because Adam was partly from Him and partly*
> *from the earth... "*

You can read the detailed discussion of this judgment in the book that I mentioned above.

The Holy Spirit is the Power in God's Breath

In **2 Samuel 22:16**, we see a scripture that that tells us about the power of the **Holy Spirit** in God's breath; it can blast the earth to pieces if God wants it to. **We must always remember that we are dealing with an awesome God who holds all the power in the universe; His voice makes the universe to tremble:**

> "And the channels of the sea appeared, the foundations of the world were discovered, <u>at the rebuking of the LORD</u>, **at the blast of the breath of his nostrils**."

This is why the Lord Jesus commanded us to fear Him because **He can scatter with His breath as well as give life with His breath.** At the same time, God can breathe His breath and people and things can become pieces of relics. Look at the so-called great empires or civilizations (from Assyria to Rome) that rose up against His people Israel; where are they now? They are in the relic books of antiquity while Israel is a thriving nation again!

The Lord Jesus Breathed the Holy Spirit on the Disciples

Again, we see the **Holy Spirit** as the **breath of God** after the death and resurrection of the Lord Jesus. He came to the disciples and He **breathed the Holy Spirit on them** saying, **"receive the Holy Ghost** *(Holy Spirit)*" in **John 20:22.** This is the beginning of the **life of God** or the breath of God that overcomes the "second death" in those who believe in

Christ and in His finished works on the Cross. **The disciples immediately became <u>born again</u> by the Holy Spirit when they received the breath of God from the Lord Jesus:**

> "And when he *(Jesus)* had said this, **he breathed on them**, and saith unto them, **Receive ye the Holy Ghost...**"

This **breath of God** is what keeps the souls of all those who believed in the atoning blood of the Lord Jesus from being eternally separated from God and forever damned in hell. The Bibles calls this "the second death." We need to always remember that the **Holy Spirit** is the **breath of life in our human spirits** and we say that a person is dead when his or her spirit returns back to God; our spirits never die. As a result, the spirits of all human beings (believers and unbelievers) return back to God at death and the bodies go back to the ground from where they were taken. It is the souls of men and women that will be judged. **The Holy Spirit is the breath giving life of God in every human being because we all came from Adam.**

Today, there are still many people on earth that have not believed in the finished works of Christ. **What they do not know is that without the breath of the Holy Spirit that God gives us when we believe in Christ; they are not spiritually alive to God.** Although they are breathing physically by the breath that was given to Adam in the Garden of Eden, they are essentially the "walking dead" in the realm of the spirit because **the day that Adam sinned, Adam died spiritually (became separated from God by sin) and all human beings inherited the spiritual death.** This is why in **Luke 9:57-60**, the Lord Jesus called the living 'dead' when He was here. You can read it here in its context:

> "And it came to pass, that, as they went in the way, <u>a certain man said unto him, Lord, I will</u>

follow thee whithersoever thou goest. *58* And Jesus said unto him, Foxes have holes, and birds of the air have nests; but the Son of man hath not where to lay his head. *59* And he said unto another, Follow me. **But he said, Lord, suffer me first to go and bury my father.** *60* Jesus said unto him, **Let the dead** *(his family; the 'living dead')* **bury their dead** *(his physically dead father)*: but go thou and preach the kingdom of God."

It is only when we come to the Lord Jesus Christ that God brings us back to life again by giving us **the breath of life**; the life of Christ through the power and workings of the **Holy Spirit**.

My Vision of the 'Living Dead'

As I have already written in one of my books titled, **Unveiling the God-mother, pages 22-27,** I took a fatal fall in my early years and died. I fell from an upstairs floor and died instantly and it was not until the next morning that someone discovered my dead body. I will not go into the details of the events here as you can read the full story in the book that I mentioned above. What I want to share here is what I saw concerning the "living dead:"

My death occurred right around 8 or 9 pm because the adults usually go to bed between 7 and 8 pm. When they are gone to bed, we the children will then sneak out to play in the full moonlight. After my fall and when my playmates realized that I was dead, they all decided to sneak back into their various houses. To their credit, they did try to revive me by shaking me several times without success before they all ran away. Because I was in the clouds above them, I could see them and all that they were doing.

It did not bother me that they were running away because I had never felt better; I could see farther than I had ever seen before. As a matter of fact, I could see the entire town! Moreover, thanks to 'my friend in the dream' who I later found out was called Jesus, I did not even feel the pain of the blow of death because He had visited me in a dream some days prior and rubbed my forehead with His hand which was the part of my body that I landed on during my fall! What shocked me was what I saw as each one of my playmates sneaked back into their houses.

I saw the members of their families as nothing but 'dead skeleton' (dead bones) on their beds and mats. I could not understand why they were all 'dead' without any flesh on them at all. Because I saw that the houses that they were sneaking back into had no 'human with flesh on them' but skeletal bones as when someone had been dead for many years, I became determined to find at least one person in a house; any house that looked human or was a real human being. I was shocked as I searched every house in the entire town and I could not find anyone. Due to the fact that I did not know anything about the Bible and the Prophet Ezekiel's vision of the Valley of the Dry Bones, I did not know what I was looking at. I was so sad that in the entire town, not one person looked human; they were just nothing but the 'living dead'. The search occupied me for the whole night into the early morning until someone discovered my dead body.

I saw firsthand what the Lord meant when **He referred to those living <u>without the life</u> that He came to give us as "dead."** We thank God for **His Word** and His **Holy Spirit**.

The Holy Spirit as the Rushing Mighty Wind

We see the **Holy Spirit** as **Wind** in **Genesis 8:1-3** after the flood in Noah's days. He was the one that made the waters to become "abated" after **God the Father** released Him over the flooded earth:

> "And God remembered Noah, and every living thing, and all the cattle that was with him in the ark: and **God made a wind** *(the Holy Spirit)* **to pass over the earth,** and **the waters asswaged;** 2 The **fountains** also of the **deep** and the **windows of heaven** were **stopped,** and the **rain from heaven was restrained;** 3 And the waters returned from off the earth continually: and after the end of the hundred and fifty days **the waters were abated.**"

The scripture above also helps us to understand what the **Holy Spirit** did in **Genesis 1:2** when **"the earth was without form and void."** It was the **Holy Spirit** who operated as **Wind** and thawed out the frozen deep so that the water became unfrozen:

> "And the earth was without form, and void; and darkness was upon the face of the deep. **And the Spirit of God moved upon the face of the waters.**"

Also, we see the **Holy Spirit** as a **"Mighty Rushing Wind"** in **Acts 2:1-2** on the Day of Pentecost when the disciples gathered together in one accord to pray and seek God:

> "And when the day of Pentecost was fully come, they were all with one accord in one place. 2 **And suddenly there came a sound from heaven as of a rushing mighty wind, and it filled all the house where they were sitting...**"

We will examine this scripture above in detail later in this chapter in a discussion of what happened on the day that the Lord Jesus was **anointed** by **God the Father** in heaven.

My Initial Ignorance about the Anointing

I remember when I newly became born again and I was in

a church service and I had an encounter with the **Anointing** and I was afraid of it because not long before, I saw a sticker on a moving vehicle that read: *The Anointing Destroys the Yoke* and the devil immediately struck fear in my heart concerning it. His words to me were, "who knows what you are getting when it comes to the anointing?" Of course, I did not know that it was the devil then but as a result of the evil thought, I told myself that I will do well not to get involved in anything that had to do with it.

One day during a church service and as the devil was trying to scare me (remember the guy with the expanding and contracting ears?) and I decided to defy him, I began to smell olive oil. The more I tried to close my nose, the stronger the smell got. It was at this time that God the Father opened heaven and I saw the vision about the **Godhead** that I narrated earlier. Prior to this day, I had no idea that God uses olive oil or that the **Holy Spirit** had any connection to olive oil. Somehow during my struggle with the smell of olive oil, I became aware that it had something to do with the **Anointing** and I was terrified. Between the awareness of the **Anointing** and the guy manifesting before me, I really needed to "walk by faith and not by sight" by confessing God's Word to that effect. Needless to say that at the end, it was comforting to learn that the **Anointing** was indeed of God and that it speaks of the **Holy Spirit**.

Just as I was initially, there are many people today that are a bit apprehensive when it comes to the **Anointing** or to the workings of the **Holy Spirit**. I have actually come across people who want to attend church services just as long as there is no "manifestation" of the **works of the Holy Spirit**. If you are one of them, I hope that reading this portion of this book will help ease your mind and remove the devil's fear tactics in your life concerning the **Anointing**. I have personally found out that the **Anointing** does indeed destroy every yoke; it destroyed every yoke that the devil wanted to afflict me with.

Therefore, I encourage you to desire it and to embrace it in your life so that you can live a victorious Christian life. The **Anointing** is for all who believe in the Lord Jesus Christ and His work on the Cross.

The Holy Spirit as the Anointing

Although <u>He is a Person</u>, the **Lord Holy Spirit** can transform or **change form** to become the **Anointing** and as the **Anointing,** you can see Him as **Oil** or **Divine Favor. The Anointing is defined as divine intervention or the oil of sanctification or consecration.** For example, to be **anointed** with God's **Anointing Oil** means to be consecrated and dedicate to the service of God. It is the **Holy Spirit** that consecrates us to the service of God. Therefore, the **Anointing Oil** is an earthly representation of the **Holy Spirit**. It speaks of the **Holy Spirit** Himself.

We were first introduced to this **Anointing or consecration** with the **Anointing Oil** during the ministry of Moses and Aaron in the wilderness on their way to the Promised Land. God commanded Moses to make the **Anointing Oil** and He gave Moses strict instructions concerning the **Anointing Oil**. Below is how God specified that the **Anointing Oil** be made in **Exodus 30:22-25:**

> "Moreover the LORD spake unto Moses, saying, 23 <u>Take thou also unto thee principal spices</u>, **of pure myrrh five hundred shekels**, and **of <u>sweet cinnamon</u> half so much**, even two hundred and fifty shekels, and **of sweet <u>calamus</u> two hundred and fifty shekels**, 24 And **of <u>cassia</u> five hundred shekels,** after the shekel of the sanctuary, and **of <u>oil olive</u> an hin: 25 And thou shalt make it an oil of holy ointment**, an ointment compound after the art of the apothecary: **it shall be an holy anointing oil.**"

After making the **Anointing Oil**, God commanded Moses in **Exodus 29:1-9** to take Aaron and his sons and **to** <u>consecrate</u> **them with the** <u>Anointing Oil</u> **so that they can stand in the 'Priest's Office' to minister to Him:**

> "And this is the thing that thou shalt do unto them to **hallow them, to minister unto me in the priest's office:** Take one young bullock, and two rams without blemish, 2 And unleavened bread, and cakes unleavened tempered with oil, and wafers unleavened **anointed with oil**...4 **And Aaron and his sons thou shalt bring unto the door of the tabernacle of the congregation, and shalt wash them with water.** 5 <u>And thou shalt take the garments, and put upon Aaron the coat, and the robe of the ephod, and the ephod, and the breastplate, and gird him with the curious girdle of the ephod:</u>
>
> 6 <u>And thou shalt put the mitre upon his head, and put the holy crown upon the mitre.</u> 7 **Then shalt thou take the** <u>anointing oil</u>, **and pour it upon his head, and** <u>anoint him</u>. 8 And thou shalt bring his sons, and put coats upon them. 9 **And thou shalt gird them with girdles, Aaron and his sons, and put the bonnets on them: and the priest's office shall be theirs for a perpetual statute:** <u>**and thou shalt** consecrate **Aaron and his sons.**</u>"

God again stressed the importance of **anointing Aaron and his sons** in **Exodus 30:30-33** and He also commanded Moses that anyone who dares to make or use the **Anointing Oil** on his or herself besides Aaron and His sons was to be put to death. That is how holy and revered the **Anointing Oil** was in the days of Moses and we too will do well to revere it:

"**And thou shalt anoint Aaron and his sons, and consecrate them, that they may minister unto me in the priest's office.** *31* And thou shalt speak unto the children of Israel, saying, **This shall be an holy anointing oil unto me throughout your generations.** *32* **Upon man's flesh shall it not be poured**, neither shall ye make any other like it, after the composition of it: it is holy, and **it shall be holy unto you.** *33* **Whosoever compoundeth any like it, or whosoever putteth any of it upon a stranger, shall even be cut off from his people** *(put to death)*."

The reason God said to put to death anyone that makes or applies the Anointing Oil to him or herself besides the Priests (Aaron and his descendants) that were ministering to Him was because the <u>Anointing Oil represents the Holy Spirit</u>. The **Holy Spirit** is not given to just anyone but to those who are consecrated to God as His priests. **This is why it was <u>necessary for Christ to make us all who believe in Him Kings and Priests unto God so that we can qualify to receive the Anointing</u>.** He successfully accomplished this task as we see in **Revelation 1:5-6:**

"And from <u>Jesus Christ</u>, who is the faithful witness, and the first begotten of the dead, and <u>the prince of the kings of the earth</u>. **Unto him that loved us, and <u>washed us from our sins in his own blood</u>,** *6* **And hath <u>made us kings and priests</u> unto God and his Father;** to him be glory and dominion forever and ever. Amen."

In Christ Jesus, we are now God's **kings** and **priests** on earth and He gives us the Anointing to consecrate us to Him.

Laying on of Hands to Transfer the Anointing

As the **Anointing**, the **Holy Spirit** is actually transferable;

meaning that you can impart Him from one believer to another. <u>You can lay hands on someone that just became born again and transfer the **Holy Spirit** (the Anointing) upon that person by laying your hands on the person.</u> **What happens is that God uses the hands of believers to fill a new believer with the Holy Spirit**. This is a very unique nature of the **Holy Spirit**; He is very transferable as the **Anointing**.

It means that you have to be b**orn again** and **sanctified by the blood of the Lord Jesus** even today before you can qualify to <u>receive</u> or <u>use</u> the **Anointing** or the **Anointing Oil**. We can see how quickly <u>Apostle Peter's rebuke struck fear and terror in the heart of Simon</u>; the <u>sorcerer</u> who had used his witchcrafts to bewitch the people of Samaria for a long time but sought to <u>buy the anointing with money</u>. Although he (Simon) was opposing the work that the disciples were doing in Samaria, he saw that the **Anointing** was being released to those who believed by the **laying on of hands** and that the disciples were performing miracles, signs and wonders with it.

Therefore, he wanted to pay Peter some money so that Peter could impart the **Anointing** to him. In other words, he wanted the glory of going around and laying hands on people to release the **Holy Spirit** and to do miracles, signs and wonders without belonging to Christ. The Apostle Peter knew that his vain desire was a colossal sin in the sight of both God and man. Read about the encounter in **Acts 8:14-24** below:

> "<u>Now when the apostles which were at Jerusalem heard that Samaria had received the word of God, they sent unto them Peter and John</u>: *15* **Who, when they were come down, prayed for them, that they might receive the Holy Ghost:** *16* (For as yet he was fallen upon none of them: only they were baptized in the name of the Lord

Jesus.) *17* **Then laid they their hands on them, and they received the Holy Ghost.**

18 **And when Simon saw that through laying on of the apostles' hands the Holy Ghost was given, he offered them money,** *19* **Saying, Give me also this power, that on whomsoever I lay hands, he may receive the Holy Ghost.** *20* But Peter said unto him, **Thy money perish with thee, because thou hast thought that the gift of God may be purchased with money.** *21* **Thou hast neither part nor lot in this matter: for thy heart is not right in the sight of God.**

22 **Repent therefore of this thy wickedness, and pray God, if perhaps the thought of thine heart may be forgiven thee.** *23* **For I perceive that thou art in the gall of bitterness, and in the bond of iniquity.** *24* Then answered Simon, and said, Pray ye to the Lord for me, that none of these things which ye have spoken come upon me."

As you can see, the **Anointing** is not given to anyone who is not yet **saved or born again** because as scriptures revealed to us, the **Anointing** is the **Holy Spirit**. In **Joel 2:28**, God promised to pour out **His Spirit** (the Anointing) upon all flesh and as a result, men, women and even the aged will receive the divine grace to dream dreams and to see visions but this promise lingered for hundred of years. **The reason that it lingered was because it could not be fulfilled until the Lord Jesus accomplished the works of our redemption with His atoning blood so that whosoever believe will receive the Anointing.**

This is how He did it according to **Hebrews 9:14-15**. When He rose again from the dead, He went into the Holy

<u>of Holies</u> by the power of the **Holy Spirit** <u>and</u> **He presented His own blood to God as payment for <u>our sin</u> (rebellion) against God:**

> **"How much more shall the blood of Christ, <u>who through the eternal Spirit</u>** *(the Holy Spirit)* **<u>offered himself without spot to God</u>, purge your conscience from dead works to serve the living God?** 15 And for this cause he is the mediator of the new testament, that by means of death, for the redemption of the transgressions that were under the first testament, they which are called might receive the promise of eternal inheritance."

He came back to earth to announce to the disciples and to us (believers) that as many as believe in what He did shall not perish but shall receive eternal life. **This is why we preach the good news of how Christ paid for all our sins and why we compel everyone to come to Him and receive eternal life and to qualify to also receive the Anointing.**

The Overflow of the Anointing Oil on Aaron and the Lord Jesus

The Bible talks about the **Anointing Oil** as the **Oil of Gladness** and as we already saw, Moses **anointed** Aaron with the **Anointing Oil** to install him as the **High Priest** to minister before God. When Aaron was **anointed** by Moses, the **Anointing Oil** (ointment) <u>flowed from Aaron's head to his beard and to the rest of his garments</u>; meaning from his head to the rest of his body as recorded in **Psalm 133:1-2:**

> "Behold, how good and how pleasant it is for brethren to dwell together in unity! 2 **It is like the precious <u>ointment</u>** *(Anointing)* **upon the head, that ran down upon the beard, even Aaron's beard: that went down to the skirts of his garments."**

Also, the day that the Lord Jesus was **Anointed** in heaven with the "**Oil of Gladness**" is the day that we call the **Day of Pentecost** on earth. What happened was that God the Father poured the **Anointing Oil** on the Lord Jesus to formally install Him as **Lord, God**, and <u>our new</u> **High Priest** in heaven as recorded in **Hebrews 1:8-12.** It is God the Father's investiture speech over His Son, the Lord Jesus Christ:

> "**But unto the Son** *(Jesus)* **he** *(God the Father)* **saith,** <u>Thy throne, O God</u>, is forever and ever: a sceptre of righteousness is the sceptre of thy kingdom. 9 Thou hast loved righteousness, and hated iniquity; therefore God, even <u>thy God</u>, hath **anointed** thee with the **oil of gladness** above thy fellows *(humanity)*.
>
> 10 And, <u>Thou, **Lord**</u> *(Jesus)*, in the beginning hast laid the foundation of the earth; and the heavens are the works of thine hands *(Jesus as the Word-'Let there be…' is the creator of the earth):* 11 They shall perish; but thou remainest; and they all shall wax old as doth a garment; 12 And as a vesture shalt thou fold them up, and they shall be changed: but thou art the same, and thy years shall not fail."

The <u>scripture in Hebrews</u> above was actually the fulfillment of the Word of God in **Psalm 45:6-8**. As you will read below, the <u>spices</u> listed in the **Anointing Oil** with which the Lord Jesus was anointed are some of <u>the same spices specified by God in the making of the</u> **Anointing Oil** of the **High Priest** in the days of Moses:

> "Thy throne, **O God** *(Jesus)*, is forever and ever: the sceptre of thy kingdom is a right sceptre. 7 Thou lovest righteousness, and hatest wickedness: therefore God, <u>thy God, hath anointed thee with the **oil of gladness** above thy fellows</u>. 8 All thy garments smell of **myrrh**,

and **aloes**, and **cassia,** out of the ivory palaces, whereby they have made thee glad."

This means that the **Lord Jesus** from the **Day of Pentecost** stands before **God the Father** in the Office of the <u>High Priest</u> to minister as **our High Priest** forever. Just as the **Anointing Oil** overflowed to Aaron's beard and garments when Moses anointed him, the **Anointing Oil** also overflowed <u>from the head of the Lord Jesus to the rest of His body</u> (the Church) and **the believers experienced that overflow on the Day of Pentecost as the outpouring of the Holy Spirit!**

In other words, on the day that the Lord Jesus received His coronation in heaven (Day of Pentecost), the **Anointing Oil** flowed from Him to the Church (His body) and the believers that were gathered together experienced the **Holy Spirit** as we see in **Acts 2:1-4:**

> "And when the **day of Pentecost** was fully come, they were all with one accord in one place. 2 And suddenly there came a sound from heaven as of **<u>a rushing mighty wind</u>, and it filled all the house where they were sitting.** 3 And **there appeared unto them <u>cloven tongues like as of fire</u>, and it sat upon each of them.** 4 And **they were all <u>filled with the Holy Ghost</u>, and began <u>to speak as the Spirit gave them utterance</u>.**"

Here you see the **Holy Spirit manifesting Himself in different ways at the same time**; <u>first</u>, He comes in as **"a mighty rushing wind,"** <u>next</u>, you see Him sitting as **"cloven tongues of fire"** on the disciples; then, He **"filled" them with Himself** and <u>finally</u>, He gave them **utterances to speak with new tongues;** <u>all at the same time!</u> He is the power of God and He is who God uses to get things done. He can do anything that God wants done and He can do an infinite number of tasks at the same time.

As the **Anointing** or the **Oil of Gladness**, the **Holy Spirit** has been with us believers on earth since the Day of Pentecost. The **Holy Spirit** is also referred to as the **Oil of Joy**. Because the Anointing Oil is also the **"Oil of Gladness,"** <u>God did not allow Aaron to mourn</u> when two of his sons (Nadab and Abihu) offered "strange incense" to God and God slew them — Leviticus 10:1-7. This is why we are not supposed to mourn or fraternize with death by going to funeral wakes to view dead bodies because it defiles the anointing. It is also why **we are <u>not</u> supposed to put ashes on our foreheads** (a sign of mourning) because the Lord has given us "beauty for ashes" and the "Oil of Gladness or Joy to overcome the spirit of heaviness." We are to do the same to those that mourn; **give them beauty for ashes:**

> "To appoint unto them that mourn in Zion, **to give unto them <u>beauty for ashes</u>, the oil of joy for mourning, the garment of praise for the spirit of heaviness;** that they might be called trees of righteousness, the planting of the LORD, that he might be glorified" (Isaiah 61:3).

We need to correct the Christians who go around with ashes on their foreheads in their celebration of "Ash Wednesday." It is a religious practice that is born out of the ignorance of the true meaning of what Jesus Christ did for us on the Cross — He gave us beauty (eternal life/ oil of gladness) for ashes. We must therefore, wear his beauty (oil of gladness) and not sorrowful ashes. He is risen from the dead and He reigns from heaven over the whole earth! Therefore, we have no more reason to be sorrowful or to mourn.

Anointing the Sick with Oil

It is the **Holy Spirit** that operates as the **Anointing** to make us effective ministers of the Gospel of Jesus Christ in order to minister healing and deliverance to all those who are afflicted by the devil and his demons. He is here to help us as we are told in **James 5:14-15:**

> "<u>Is any sick among you? let him call for the elders of the church; and let them pray over him,</u> **anointing him with oil in the name of the Lord:** 15 And the prayer of faith shall save the sick, and the Lord shall raise him up; and if he have committed sins, they shall be forgiven him."

As God's king and priests in Christ, we should boldly operate the ministry that the Lord Jesus has given us by using the **Anointing Oil** to heal the sick.

My Vision of the Holy Spirit as the Anointing

*I have been privileged by God to see the **Holy Spirit** as the **Anointing** in heaven. He sits as **a person** and yet, **He is in a liquid form of oil** and when I looked at Him closely, I saw Him as a very clean and clear golden oil. I also saw that He was endlessly pouring Himself out as this golden oil upon the entire earth. I watched Him to the point that the earth was almost completely saturated with Him as this golden oil and yet, He was not diminished in size or shape! Although He was gushing Himself out like a mighty river of oil upon the earth, His size did not change and I was amazed.*

His size remains the same in the same ways as when I saw the Lord Jesus Christ also. I saw the Lord Jesus receiving believers from all over the world into Himself without also increasing in size! In the vision, the Lord Jesus was standing with His hands held up high in a prayer form and lots and lots of people from different people groups and from different nations were just entering into Him at lightning speed. I mean; millions of people and His size did *not change. It was amazing to see the **Holy Spirit** as the Anointing and the Lord Jesus Christ as our habitation by the power of the **Holy Spirit**. Our God is truly awesome.*

The Holy Spirit as Fire

Our first glimpse of the **Holy Spirit** as **fire** was at the "burning bush." Moses saw an unusual sight; a unique occurrence in which a fire was burning in a bush but the bush was not being consumed by the fire. Moses decided to go closer to inspect the sight in **Exodus 3:2-4:**

> "And the angel of the LORD appeared unto him in **a flame of fire** out of the midst of a bush: and he looked, and, **behold, the bush burned with <u>fire</u>, and the bush was not consumed.** 3 And Moses said, I will now turn aside, and see <u>this great sight</u>, **why the bush is not burnt.** 4 And when the LORD saw that he turned aside to see, **God called unto him out of the midst of the bush**, and said, Moses, Moses. And he said, Here am I."

In this encounter, Moses did not realize that the **fire** he was beholding was actually the Spirit of God; the **Holy Spirit**! In my book titled, ***Experiencing the Depths Jesus Christ***, I wrote above this very encounter that Moses had with the **Angel of the Lord** who was in fact none other than the **Lord Jesus Christ**. Here you see **Jesus** as the **Angel of the Lord** (the express image of God) and as God. You also see the **Holy Spirit** as fire. You need to read the book on the Lord Jesus that I mentioned above because in it I explained many things that God showed me. **The Holy Spirit has been working together with the Lord Jesus in God's salvation plan to bring man back to God.**

Also, when <u>John the Baptist</u> talked about the **Lord Jesus**, he informed his audience that when He shall appear as the

Messiah; the Lord shall baptize the people with the **Holy Spirit** and with **Fire** — **Matthew 3:11:**

> "Indeed I baptize you with water unto repentance: **but he that cometh after me is mightier than I, whose shoes I am not worthy to bear: he shall <u>baptize you</u> with the <u>Holy Ghost</u>, and with <u>fire</u>.**"

As a fulfillment of what John the Baptized prophesied, the Lord Jesus baptized His Church with the **Holy Spirit** and with **Fire** on the Day of Pentecost. **Since then, it is the Holy Spirit that sets us on fire concerning the things of God so that we can go forth and boldly proclaim the truth of the Word of God.** God's Word is as fire that can be "shut up" in our very being so that we do not become complacent about the things of God.

Also, we are told in **Malachi 4:1-3** that when the Lord comes He shall refine and purify us with fire:

> "Behold, I will send my messenger, and he shall prepare the way before me: and the Lord, whom ye seek, shall suddenly come to his temple, even the messenger of the covenant, whom ye delight in: behold, he shall come, saith the LORD of hosts. 2 But who may abide the day of his coming? And who shall stand when he appeareth? **for he is like a refiner's fire, and like fullers' soap: 3 And he shall sit as a refiner and purifier of silver: and he shall purify the sons of Levi, and purge them as gold and silver, that they may offer unto the LORD an offering in righteousness.**"

The Holy Spirit as Water

The **Holy Spirit** and the Word of God have the qualities of **water** to cleanse the impurities and the ugliness in us concerning the things of God. Therefore, God uses both **His Spirit** and **His Word** to wash us of the evil that contaminated us from the devil. As a result, scriptures sometimes refer to both the **Holy Spirit** and the **Word of God** as **water**. Below is an example in **John 7:37-39:**

> "In the last day, that great day of the feast, Jesus stood and cried, saying, If any man thirst, let him come unto me, and drink. 38 **He that believeth on me, as the scripture hath said, out of his belly shall flow <u>rivers of living water.</u>** *39* (**<u>But this spake he of the Spirit, which they that believe on him should receive: for the Holy Ghost was not yet given;</u>** because that Jesus was not yet glorified.)"

When the **Lord Jesus** was making this appeal in Jerusalem on the great day of the feast, He knew that all who choose to believe in Him will be filled with the **Holy Spirit** and that the **Holy Spirit** will flow in their belly as "living waters" just as a river flows. Do you remember that He made this same appeal to the lady at the well in John Chapter 4 after He asked her to give Him water to drink?

The lady immediately reminded Him of how that the Jews have no dealings with the Samaritans. In response, the Lord told her that if she knew who she was talking to, she would have asked Him and He would have given her "living water" so that she will never thirst again. Upon hearing this, the lady assumed that He was talking about physical water but He informed her that He was talking about the **<u>water</u> (the Holy Spirit)** that produces everlasting life:

> "Jesus answered and said unto her, Whosoever drinketh of this water shall thirst again: 14 **But whosoever drinketh of <u>the water that I shall give him shall never thirst;</u> but the water that I shall give him shall be in him a well of water**

springing up into everlasting life. 15 The woman saith unto him, Sir, give me this water, that I thirst not, neither come hither to draw" (John 4:13-15).

The Holy Spirit as Inspiration

Every inspiration that we receive from God concerning Himself and His Word; the Lord Jesus, comes to us through and by the **Holy Spirit**. The Bibles tells us in **2 Timothy 3:16-17** that:

> "All scripture is given by inspiration *(the Holy Spirit)* of God**, and is profitable for doctrine, for reproof, for crrection, for instruction in righteousness: 17 That the man of God may be perfect, thoroughly furnished unto all good works."

We also saw earlier in **Acts 2:4** that the disciples spoke as the **Spirit** gave them utterances after they were filled with the **Holy Spirit:**

> "And they were **all filled with the Holy Ghost, and began to speak with other tongues, as the Spirit gave them utterance**."

As a result of these various ways in which the **Holy Spirit** manifests Himself, we can clearly see that the **Holy Spirit** is indeed the part of the Godhead that changes form. **God the Father** is true to His Word, "I am the Lord; I change not." He does not change except that He works by the power of His own Spirit; the **Holy Spirit** in various forms.

Chapter 3
The Holy Spirit is the Revelatory Side of God

He Reveals God the Father and the Lord Jesus to Us

Scriptures tells us in **John 1:18** that <u>no man has seen God at anytime</u>, but by the power of the **Holy Spirit**, the Lord Jesus was able to reveal **God the Father** to us:

> **"No man hath seen God at any time;** <u>**the only begotten Son**</u>**,** which is in the bosom of the Father, **he hath declared him."**

It was the **Holy Spirit** that helped to facilitate the ministry of the Lord Jesus while He was here on earth as a man. **God the Father** was in heaven while the Lord Jesus was operating His ministry on earth but with the help of the **Holy Spirit**, He was able to help us put a face to God. Also, with the help of the **Holy Spirit**, He was able to demonstrate the love of God to us with healings, miracles, signs and wonders. Even today, what we know of **God the Father** and the **Lord Jesus** is what the **Holy Spirit** reveals to us about them.

He is Our Teacher

It takes the **Holy Spirit** to help us understand the <u>things of God</u> as stated in **1 Corinthians 2:12-13**:

> **"Now we have received, not the spirit of the world, but** <u>**the spirit which is of God;**</u> that we might know the things that are freely given to us of God. 13 <u>Which things also we speak, not in</u> the **words which man's wisdom teacheth,** but which <u>**the Holy Ghost teacheth;**</u> **comparing spiritual things with spiritual."**

God has given us so many things in His Son, Jesus Christ but <u>these things are hidden in His Word</u>. Therefore, it is the **Holy Spirit** that will activate the Words of the Lord for us so that we can understand what God has given to us or what God wants us to know. The Epistles (Romans thru Jude) are filled with what God did for us in Christ and they also tell us what God has already made each and every one of us to become in Christ. As a new believer, when you study the Word of God; especially the Epistles, you will begin to discover by the help of the **Holy Spirit** how these things relate to you in particular.

For example, it is in the Epistles that you discover that you are now an heir of God, you have put on Christ, you are one with God and the **Holy Spirit** in Christ, you are God's ambassador, you are God's building, you have the mind of Christ, you are unblameable, you are unreproveable, etc. God wants you to take hold of all the things that He has made you and that He has given you so that you can live a victorious life and fulfill His call upon your life. One of the ways that the **Holy Spirit** will empower you in this regard is to help you to grow in spiritual discernment and this will happen as you seek Him for spiritual understanding.

As you saw in I Corinthians 2:13 above, the things of God cannot be understood by human intellect — *"Which things also we speak, not in the words which <u>man's wisdom</u> teacheth, but which the Holy Ghost teacheth; comparing spiritual things with spiritual."* Therefore, we all need the discernment that the **Holy Spirit** gives as we discipline ourselves to study the Word of God. The disciples' "spiritual eyes of understanding were opened" on the day that they were filled with the **Holy Spirit**. They then began to understand both the scriptures and the ways of God. For example, the Lord Jesus spoke to the disciples about many things but most of the time, what He said to them went over their heads.

As a result, they often wondered what He was talking about but after the Lord rose again from the dead, He gave them the baptism of the **Holy Spirit.** The Bible tells us that the Lord used the power of the **Holy Spirit** that He had given to them to <u>open their understanding</u> and they began to know the meaning of scriptures — **Luke 24:36-47:**

> "And as they thus spake, Jesus himself stood in the midst of them, and saith unto them, Peace be unto you. 37 But they were terrified and affrighted, and supposed that they had seen a spirit. 38 And he said unto them, Why are ye troubled? and why do thoughts arise in your hearts? 39 Behold my hands and my feet, that it is I myself: handle me, and see; for a spirit hath not flesh and bones, as ye see me have. 40 And when he had thus spoken, he shewed them his hands and his feet. 41 And while they yet believed not for joy, and wondered, he said unto them, Have ye here any meat?
>
> 42 And they gave him a piece of a broiled fish, and of an honeycomb. 43 And he took it, and did eat before them. And he said unto them, <u>These are the words which I spake unto you, while I was yet with you, that all things must be fulfilled, which were written in the law of Moses, and in the prophets, and in the psalms, concerning me.</u> 45 **Then opened he their understanding, that they might understand the scriptures,** 46 And said unto them, Thus it is written, and thus it behoved Christ to suffer, and to rise from the dead the third day: 47 And that repentance and remission of sins should be preached in his name among all nations, beginning at Jerusalem."

Because they did not have the **Holy Spirit** before the death of the Lord, they missed the whole purpose of why the Lord Jesus went to the Cross. Due to this ignorance, they all went with Peter to become fishermen; even the ones that had never fished before! Here is a paraphrase of what must have happened: Peter must have said, "Ok guys, Jesus is gone and we do not know what became of Him, so I am going back to my old profession which is fishing." The other disciples said, "Hey, we will go with you." By default, even the tax collector; Matthew became a fisherman along with the others. The Cross and everything that happened to the Lord Jesus did not make sense to them because it takes the **Holy Spirit** to help us understand it; He gives us discernment about it.

Without the **Holy Spirit**, the ways of God will not make sense to anyone of us. This is why **1 Corinthians 2:14** says that the unbelievers cannot receive the things of the Spirit of God because they are foolishness to them. In other words, the ways of God do not make sense to those who do not believe in Christ; especially when it comes to the Gospel. For instance, God chose to save us by what seems to the highly educated or the prestigious: a **foolish thing** to do — preaching; going around telling people that they need to be born again:

> **"But the natural man receiveth not the things of the Spirit of God: for they are foolishness unto him:** neither can he know them, **because they are spiritually discerned."**

The natural man or the man or woman that is not yet born again looks at the things of God as superstitious beliefs, archaic ways or the foolish ways of the ignorant. Worst still, if they have a better place in society or are well to do, they will view the things of God as something the poor and the unlearned hold onto. On the other hand, the Bible says that God uses the foolishness of preaching the Gospel to save those who believe and also to confound those who think they are wise; He uses the foolish things to confound the wise. It seems foolish for someone who did not seem to be doing very well in life, to tell someone who seems to be very affluent in life that he or she needs to make a change in life but it is the way that God set it up.

Below is one of my personal experiences during my preaching of the Gospel. In general, a lot of people received the message but some had disdain for me while others had contempt. Some of the 'well-to-do' people laughed at or mocked me.

My Personal Experience

The worst reaction in "street ministry" that I ever received was from a fellow African lady. It happened some years ago when my car broke down and I had to take the train to work while it was being fixed. I blamed the devil for attacking my car because I was coming back from a night of witnessing when all of a sudden my car went dead. To make matters worse, the mechanic messed up the engine while trying to fix it. He promised me a replacement engine but he had to order it from Japan and according to him, it will take at least two months to arrive by ship. I decided that if the devil was going to mess with my car, I was going to mess with him in the place where I can do him the most damage – snatch souls from him! I chose to make good use of my two months on the trains and buses so, I ordered a box of Gospel tracks to hand out as I ministered to and from work on public transportation.

One day I met this very well dressed lady from Africa at the Five Points Train Station and I proceeded to tell her that the Lord loves her. As I tried to give her a Gospel track, she looked at me from my head to my toe and she looked me over again. I knew that I too was very well dressed so she was not looking at me as a shabbily dressed person. As I watched her, I can tell that she was just disgusted by what I was doing – preaching the Gospel at a train station instead of making better use of myself. After looking me up and down in disgust, she drew a long hiss and she turned abruptly and walked away from me.

On my part and based on what some other people have said to me before, I concluded that she thought; how can someone like you come all the way from Africa and you could not find anything better to do with yourself and this is what you are doing – preaching at the train station! To her, it did not make any sense for someone to come all the way from Africa and go to school only to stand at the train

> *station telling people to be "born again." She made it plain*
> *that she was ashamed of what I was doing.*

I did not judge or blame those who judge me because it only confirmed what God's Word says in **2 Corinthians 6:3-10** about those who preach the Gospel:

> "Giving no offence in anything, that the ministry be not blamed: 4 But in all things approving ourselves as the ministers of God, in much patience, in afflictions, in necessities, in distresses, 5 In stripes, in imprisonments, in tumults, in labours, in watchings, in fastings...
>
> 9 As unknown, and yet well known; as dying, and, behold, we live; as chastened, and not killed; 10 As sorrowful, yet always rejoicing; **as poor, yet making many rich; as having nothing, and yet possessing all things.**"

As ministers of the Gospel, we know that God chose to use the "foolishness" of preaching the Gospel to save the lost and we are not ashamed of it. It is also the **Holy Spirit** that helps us to understand how God operates.

What this says to us as believers is that we cannot operate our Christian lives independent of the **Holy Spirit**. **We should involve the Holy Spirit in everything that we do.** There are some preachers that make fun of Christians who ask the **Lord Holy Spirit** what to wear or what to eat but what they fail to realize is that if you cultivate the habit of asking the **Lord Holy Spirit** questions or of communicating with Him on a daily basis, you will develop a strong <u>interactive relationship</u> with Him. Therefore, asking the **Lord Holy Spirit** what to wear or what to eat can be your starting point. You can say to Him, "**Lord Holy Spirit**, what should I wear to glorify you today or what should I do about this situation?"

I am saying this because I know from experience that when you involve the **Holy Spirit** in your daily activities, before you know it, you and the **Holy Spirit** will develop a very close relationship. As a result, you can hear His instructions in just about everything. I tell people all the time that as a new Christian, it was my desire to hear the voice of the Lord very clearly so when I read 2 Kings 4:15-37 about the Prophet Elijah who stayed at the house of the Shunammite woman and what happened when the Shunammite's son died, I was challenged to desire to hear God for myself in a similar way if not better. The Prophet Elijah's relationship with the Lord helped to encourage me in that challenge because I read that the Prophet Elijah was shocked to hear that the woman's son had died and God did not show it to him!

The **Holy Spirit** wants to alert us to what is going on around us. This is why there are times that you might know something but you do not realize that you know it by divine revelation but as you find yourself in the midst of the situation, the **Holy Spirit** then reminds you that this is what He was referring to when He gave you the awareness, dream or vision earlier. God does not want us to walk in ignorance and it is the reason why the Lord Jesus said in **John 8:12** that he that walks with Him does not walk in darkness:

> "Then spake Jesus again unto them, saying, **I am the light of the world: he that followeth me shall not walk in darkness, but shall have the light of life.**"

It is a direct challenge for every Christian to learn to walk with the **Holy Spirit** and involve Him in the little things that he or she does. I personally found out that the **Holy Spirit** also desires that we involve Him in our daily activities. This is how it happened:

When I was living with my brother, he also had a male friend as a roommate and they would use the kitchen sink and close the faucet so tight that I sometimes find it very difficult to open. Sometimes, I called on one of them to help me open the faucet but all of that changed as my communication with the Lord was growing to include my daily activities.

*One day, when I was struggling in my attempt to open the faucet, I saw my brother's roommate walking by and I said to him, "Please, can you come over here to..." but before I could finish the sentence, I heard the **Holy Spirit** saying in a very slighted and wounded way, "But, you did not ask me." I said to Him, "I am sorry Lord" and I told my brother's roommate to disregard my call for help. To my amazement, after asking the Lord to help me open the faucet, all I had to do was place my hand on it and gave it a light turn and it just opened! I decided to call on the Lord for other things as well.*

Do not let anyone tell you that when you ask for the **Holy Spirit**'s help about seemingly mundane things on a daily basis that you are being super spiritual. Let such people rely on the arm of flesh but you should be bold to move on with the **Holy Spirit**.

A word of caution here: What I have just discussed is not a license to become strange and to begin ascribing truly "spooky spiritual" stuff to the **Holy Spirit**. Avoid seeing everything under the sun as a sign from heaven. For example, I have spoken with Christians who want to know the meaning of seeing a bird on their front porch or front door. You can only ascribe meanings to these types of occurrences when you are being led by the **Holy Spirit** or directed by Him to do so. Do not spiritualize everything but always remember for example, that birds fly and sometimes, they land in places that we do not want them to; it is neither God nor the devil that puts them up to it.

He is Our Helper

The Holy Spirit is our Allos Parakletos; the Greek word for "Our Comforter." He comforts us and He empowers us to do whatever God tells us to do. Because He is sent by the Father to walk alongside us and help us, He does not do it all for us but He gives us the ability that will help us accomplish any task.

For instance, when God tells you to go give the Word of the Lord in a Christian gathering, your knees may begin to buckle, your heart may begin to pound and you may be thinking, "Oh, my God, how am I going to face all these people and speak Your Word to them?" But, when you know that you have the **Holy Spirit** with you and in you, all you have to do is call on the **Holy Spirit** and request His help and He will immediately help you not to be afraid but you will still need to go out there and speak to the people. Remember that He is sent to help you.

He Shows Us the Mysteries in God's Word

The Word of God is the only truth that there is in the entire universe and we also learned in **1 Corinthians 2:7-8** that God in His Wisdom hid in His Word, not just the mystery of the **Godhead, but also the mystery of His kingdom, kingdom principles and plans.** Therefore, it takes the **Holy Spirit** for anyone to get spiritual discernment into God's Word and God's kingdom:

> "But **we speak the wisdom of God in a mystery, even the hidden wisdom,** which God ordained before the world unto our glory: 8 **Which none of the princes of this world knew: for had they known it, they would not have crucified the Lord of glory."**

Again, the **Holy Spirit** is the one that the Lord Jesus said was going to help us understand the things of God because the things of God are coded in mystery and it will take the **Holy Spirit** to decode them. This is why the devil could not understand what was written in the Word of God concerning the Lord Jesus and the Cross. In other words, the devil did not know the reasons why **God the Father** sent the Lord Jesus into the earth and he did not know the significance of Jesus' going to the Cross. According to the scripture above, had the devil known, there was no way that he would have fallen into that trap of losing it all by sending the Lord Jesus to the Cross.

The mysteries in God's Word can only be revealed by the **Holy Spirit**. We see this in the case of the Apostle Paul in **Ephesians 3:2-6:**

> **"If ye have heard of the dispensation of the grace of God which is given me to you-ward:** 3 **How that by revelation he made known unto me the mystery;** (as I wrote afore in few words, 4 Whereby, when ye read, ye may understand my knowledge in the mystery of Christ) 5 **Which in other ages was not made known unto the sons of men, as it is now revealed unto his holy apostles and prophets by the Spirit;** 6 That the Gentiles should be fellow heirs, and of the same body, and partakers of his promise in Christ by the gospel."

He Helps Us to Study the Word of God

As a lot of people are already aware of, I wound up in a psychiatric hospital because I was being harassed in the mind by the devil and his wicked demons. After I came out of the psychiatric hospital, I went back to Nigeria for deliverance and I began a six months intense Bible Study at the church. There, I discovered that truly God is His Word and His Word is power. By the help of the **Holy Spirit, I began to understand the Bible because He taught me that when I go to read the Bible, I should always ask Him to help me understand what I read and to also help me to remember it.** He did this for me because He saw that the devil was bombarding my mind every time I try to study the Bible. I understood very quickly that I needed the Word of God to dwell richly in my mind and in my spirit. He has never disappointed me because He helps me each time and if I need to remember something that I had read, I simply ask Him to help me remember it.

I have met some people who say that when they read scriptures, they cannot remember what they have read. I usually tell them what the Lord taught me; meaning that before they read any scripture in the future, they should always call on the **Holy Spirit** to teach them scriptures and to help them remember them afterwards. When you ask Him, He will come to your aid because I know from experience that He loves to have a good student in His one-on-one classroom. He is glad when you want to learn some things from Him because He knows that the knowledge He gives you will empower you.

I have also learned that if you want to calm your mind and your spirit, you need the Word of God. For example, if you do not read your Bible all the time, you will have all kinds of warfare in your mind. The one thing that can subdue the human mind is the Word of God. The more you get away from the Bible and spend your time outside the Word of God, the more your mind is available for demons to debate with you, wrestle with you, or "chit chat" with you about everything that they want you to focus on. In their attempt to distract you, they will engage your mind with unnecessary thoughts and you will find yourself always binding demonic thoughts instead of being at peace in your mind. Every Christian needs to learn how to use the Word of God to calm his or her mind and spirit.

As I stated before in another book *(Unveiling the God-mother)*, **God the Father** wanted me to know the power of His Living Word. He also wanted me to know that Him and His Word are one; so one day, I was studying the Word of God and I came to the scripture in **Proverbs 11:30** that says, "*He* *that winneth souls is wise."* In broad daylight and before my eyes, the **W** in <u>wise</u> **by the power of the Holy Spirit** lifted itself off the page of my Bible and before I knew it, it began to form into a human face and I watched as **God the Father's face** rose up from my Bible and was smiling at me from the open page of my Bible! He continued to smile as He says to me, *"I told you that I and my Word are one."*

All these happened by the revelatory power of the **Holy Spirit**. God wanted me to know that the Bible was not just a literature book. With this experience, I saw that God can actually activate His Word by His **Holy Spirit** to someone that needed to know Him. There is no way that human wisdom can help anyone understand God or His Word. Those who have tried have only misled themselves and others. God has so many wonderful things laid up for us that believe in what He did for us in Christ Jesus. One of the reasons why the Lord Jesus so willingly went to die a horrible death on the Cross was for us to receive what God has prepared for us. The minute we receive the baptism of the **Holy Spirit**, He begins to reveal them to us according to **1 Corinthians 2:9-11:**

> <u>"But as it is written, Eye hath not seen, nor ear heard, neither have entered into the heart of man, the things which God hath prepared for them that love him.</u> *10* **But God hath revealed them unto us by his Spirit: for the Spirit searcheth all things, yea, the deep things of God.** *11* For what man knoweth the things of a man, save the spirit of man which is in him? <u>**even so the things of God knoweth no man, but the Spirit of God**</u>."

Therefore, we must rely on the **Holy Spirit** to <u>reveal</u> the things of God to us.

To see how badly we need the guidance and teaching of the **Holy Spirit**, read **Matthew 16:21-23** and note the following encounter between Peter and the Lord. **It will show**

you how our good intentions outside of the will of God can ignorantly make us the devil's ally. When the Lord informed the disciples that He was going to Jerusalem and that He was going to be delivered to the Gentiles, scourged and killed, Peter, one of His disciples took Him aside and rebuked Him saying that these things will never happen. Peter made the statement not knowing the purpose of the Cross or why the Lord had to go to the Cross but the Lord knew that it was satan that was talking through Peter. Peter's statement was against the will of God so it made him the devils ally in this case. Therefore, the Lord Jesus had to rebuke the spirit (satan) that was speaking through Peter to Him. He told satan to get behind Him because our inspirations are either from God or from the devil:

> "From that time forth began Jesus to shew unto his disciples, how that he must go unto Jerusalem, and suffer many things of the elders and chief priests and scribes, and be killed, and be raised again the third day. 22 **Then Peter took him, and began to rebuke him, saying, Be it far from thee, Lord: this shall not be unto thee.** 23 But he turned, and said unto Peter, **Get thee behind me, Satan: thou art an offence unto me: for thou savourest not the things that be of God, but those that be of men.**"

We desperately need the **Holy Spirit** to reveal God to us and to teach us the things of God. Without Him, we are in the dark concerning the things of God.

He Helps Us Know When God Has Moved on Our Behalf

We that believe God's Word and wait patiently for it to be manifested or fulfilled in our lives, **need the Holy Spirit to help us to know when God has moved or is about to move on our behalf.** To accomplish this, He uses visions, dreams, Words of Knowledge, Words of Wisdom and the Inner Witness (conscience) to speak to us. We find a good example of this in **Luke 2:25-32** about <u>a devoted man of God called Simeon who fasted and waited patiently for God to fulfill His Word concerning the Messiah being born in his lifetime</u>. God informed him by the **Holy Spirit** that the Messiah had been born and that He was at the temple to be circumcised. This information from the **Holy Spirit** prompted Simeon to go to the Temple to see God's Word to him fulfilled:

> "And, behold, there was a man in Jerusalem, whose name was Simeon; and the same man was just and devout, waiting for the consolation of Israel: and the Holy Ghost was upon him. 26 **And it was revealed unto him by the <u>Holy Ghost</u>, that he should not see death, before he had seen the Lord's Christ. 27 And he came by the Spirit into the temple**: and when the parents brought in the child Jesus, to do for him after the custom of the law,

> 28 Then took he him up in his arms, and blessed God, and said, 29 Lord, now lettest thou thy servant depart in peace, according to thy word: 30 **For mine eyes have seen thy salvation,** 31 Which thou hast prepared before the face of all people; 32 A light to lighten the Gentiles, and the glory of thy people Israel."

The same thing happened to a woman named Anna who was also expecting the arrival of the Messiah. She was also informed by the **Holy Spirit** that the Messiah had been born and was at the temple. Many of us receive visions and dreams from the **Holy Spirit** to this effect also. There are those who receive visitations or manifestations of the Lord in their times of need or hopelessness. He does these things because He loves us and He wants to encourage us.

Chapter 4
He is the Source of Our New Birth

The Lord Jesus said in **John 3:3-8:**

> "...**Verily, verily, I say unto thee, Except a man be born again, he cannot** <u>see</u> **the kingdom of God.** 4 Nicodemus saith unto him, How can a man be born when he is old? can he enter the second time into his mother's womb, and be born? 5 **Jesus answered, Verily, verily, I say unto thee, Except a man be born of** <u>water</u> **and of** <u>the Spirit</u>, **he cannot enter into the kingdom of God.**
>
> 6 <u>That which is born of the flesh is flesh; and that which is born of the Spirit is spirit</u>. 7 Marvel not that I said unto thee, **Ye must be born again. 8 The wind bloweth where it listeth, and thou hearest the sound thereof, but canst not tell whence it cometh, and whither it goeth**: <u>*so is every one that is born of the Spirit*</u>."

As you can clearly see from the scripture above, no one can be born again apart from the **Holy Spirit**. Therefore, we that are Christians believe <u>without any doubt</u> that the **Holy Spirit** is the source of our new birth in Christ Jesus. In the Lord's own Words in the scripture above, *"that which is born of the flesh is flesh; and that which is born of the Spirit is spirit."* The Lord again emphasized our need to be born again by saying, *"Marvel not that I said unto thee,* <u>*Ye must*</u> *be born again...?"* **Being born again** is therefore **a must for all of us** and it cannot be circumvented in the path to becoming a Christian. There is no other way of getting to God except to be born again by the **Holy Spirit** in Christ.

The Lord then went on to explain to us the <u>special nature</u> of the **Holy Spirit** by saying that, *"The wind bloweth where it listeth, and thou hearest the sound thereof, but canst not tell whence* *it cometh, and whither it goeth."* **According to Him, it is the same way when we are born of the Holy Spirit; we cannot pinpoint or explain how it happened.** In other words, the ways of the Spirit cannot be predetermined or placed in a bottle but it is just as on the Day of Pentecost when the **Holy Spirit** suddenly blew into the room where the disciples were. How He comes is determined by Him; if He wants to make noise, He can make noise or He can just rest on your head as fire or as the Anointing.

This is why when people make programs, plans or events in their churches, they sometimes can schedule the **Holy Spirit** out of the them because they do not leave Him room to come in and do whatever it is that God wants done. Their programs make no room for anything that was not listed on their agenda to happen. Therefore, we must always remember that the ways of the **Holy Spirit** cannot be predetermined.

The Holy Spirit Helps Us to Communicate With God

Something happens <u>in us</u> spiritually when we become born again by the **Holy Spirit**. This is another reason why the Lord said that *"so is every one that is born of the Spirit."* **The Holy Spirit gives our human spirit the ability to communicate with God the Father and the Lord Jesus when we become one with Christ.** This is why sometimes when you are praying or worshipping God, He can give you visions and spiritual awareness and He can catch you up and take you to heaven. While there, He will enable you to behold the glorious beauty of the Father's face and of heaven. In heaven, **God the Father** or the **Lord Jesus** can talk with you and give you instructions personally.

As for me, there have been times when I was in prayer or worshiping the Lord and in a twinkling of an eye, I find myself in space far above the earth and in the midst of the stars. I will look down on the earth as I am going up and the earth is nothing but a globe just the way that the astronauts see it when they are in space. Other times, as I open my mouth to pray and say "Father," He says, "Oh, daughter," and right there, I find myself in heaven with Him. All of these things happen at the will of the **Holy Spirit** because our going and our coming are determined <u>by the will of the Lord</u> through the **Holy Spirit**.

What I am saying is that although you are a human being, once you become born again, God can begin to use His Spirit to show you things on earth and in heaven and He can take you there personally. For instance, there are times that some people think that they are seeing things in dreams or in night visions but some of them are actually visitations in which God catches them up and takes them to those places or even to heaven. They wake up and their experiences feel very real but what they are not aware of is that they were actually taken by the **Holy Spirit** to those places.

The Prophet Ezekiel is a very good example of a prophet that used to be caught up by the hair on His head and taken from one place to another by the **Holy Spirit**. This happened to the Prophet Ezekiel in the physical and yet, Ezekiel was not born again; so how much more we that are now born of the Spirit of God. In the twinkling of an eye, God can catch you up and take you to wherever He wants to take you in order to show you whatever He wants to show you.

God the Father Wanted a Higher Birth for Us

On numerous times the Lord Jesus made a public appeal for "whosoever will" to come to Him and He made it clear that whoever believes in Him receives eternal life and the **Holy Spirit** because it is the **Holy Spirit** that makes a difference in our Christian walk. **Everyone that is on planet earth was born of a woman but God desires a higher birth for us; to be born of His own Spirit so that we can be a part of Him** — *"Being born again, not of corruptible seed, but of incorruptible, by the <u>word of God</u>, which liveth and abideth forever"* —**1 Peter 1:23. To be born of a woman <u>only</u> is a lower birth that separates man from God but to be**

born of the Spirit of God is to be united with God. This is why the Lord Jesus told the Jews of His days in **Matthew 11:11** that of <u>all those born of women</u>, there have not arisen one greater than John the Baptist <u>but that the least in the kingdom of God is greater than John the Baptist</u>:

> "Verily I say unto you, <u>Among them that are born of women there hath not risen a greater than John the Baptist</u>: **notwithstanding he that is least in the kingdom of heaven is greater than he.**"

To be born of a woman is to be born of flesh and blood <u>only</u> but when we are born again, we are born of the Spirit of God; a higher birth. Because of this higher birth, when you look at yourself as the "new creation" in the realm of the spirit, you will be amazed at how glorious you look and at how you have actually put on Jesus Christ as your covering! You will see that you are now definitely different from the "you" that you see in the physical every day. This happened because you have been born again by the Spirit of God:

> "<u>For as many of you as have been baptized into Christ</u> *(born again)* **have put on Christ**" (Galatians 3:27).

We actually put on Christ just as Adam and Eve put on the skin of the lamb that **God the Father** sacrificed in the Garden of Eden to cover their sin. The scripture tells us that that Lamb that God slew in the garden was Christ. This is why He is called the Lamb that was slain from the foundation of the world in **Revelation 13:8:**

> "…Whose names are not written in the book of life of the Lamb **slain from the foundation of the world.**"

It is not enough to go to church every time the doors open or work hard in the service of God inside and outside of Church, but <u>you must make sure that you are born again by</u>

the Spirit of God. There are many people who are serving God but who do not know Him or truly belong to Him because they have not been born again. The Lord illustrated this point to me in a night vision using a cruise ship that was docked at a seaport. If you have ever been on a cruise or on a shore excursion, you will understand what it is like for a ship to dock in a seaport. You can read it below:

Night Vision of a 'Cruise Ship'

In this vision, there was a very huge ship that looked like a 'Cruise Ship' that was docked at a seaport. Many of the passengers were on shore and as I looked closely, I saw that some of the people had decided to make BBQ on grills, some were in the deep blue waters swimming in their swim suits, some were taking pictures, some were just standing around talking and some were on the deck of the ship.

As I continued to look, I saw a woman that I happen to know in real life and she was moving from one group of people to another tuking pictures and asking for her picture to be taken with them. She seemed to me as one of the passengers on the ship but the Lord spoke to me and informed me that she was not a registered passenger on the ship but she thinks and acts as though she was. He said that she represents people who go to church and participate in most of the activities in the church without getting to know Him or taking the necessary steps to be born again so that they can belong to Him.

According to Him, the ship is just like Noah's Ark (Jesus) and all those who are born again are registered passengers in it but those who are drifting in and out of it and treating their Christian life like a picnic are going to be surprised on the day of rapture to learn that they are not registered passengers in the Ark that the Lord Jesus represents.

I narrated the night vision above to you in order to let you know that you need to be born of the Spirit of God so that you can legally and spiritually belong to Christ. Remember that the scriptures say in **Romans 8:9** that if any man has not the **Spirit of Christ**; meaning the **Holy Spirit**, that man does not belong to Christ:

> "But ye are not in the flesh, but in the Spirit, if so be that the Spirit of God dwell in you. **Now if any man have not the Spirit of Christ, he is none of his.**"

In other words, you do not belong to the Lord Jesus Christ if the **Spirit of God** does not dwell in you or if you have not been born again by the **Holy Spirit** in Christ Jesus. What am I talking about? I mean that if for instance the Lord Jesus was to appear today (rapture), a lot of people that think that they belong to Him will be shocked to find out when they are left behind that they did not obey God's Word to become born again of His Spirit and that as a result, they were not suitable candidates for rapture.

The Holy Spirit Gives Us a New Nature in Christ

The **Holy Spirit** gives us a new nature when we are born again. Therefore, one of the reasons why some people will not be raptured with the truly born again Christians is because they have not acquired the **new nature** in Christ that can live in heaven. **This new nature in Christ is critical to living in heaven because the scriptures say in 1 Corinthians 15:50-53 that flesh and blood cannot inherit eternal life.** The only blood in heaven is the blood of the Lord Jesus Christ that made atonement for our sins and it is on the Mercy Seat! By the power of the **Holy Spirit**, the Lord Jesus collected all His blood and took it to heaven; into the Holy of Holies to present it to **God the Father** as atonement for our sins. As a result, His blood is the only blood in heaven:

> "**Now this I say, brethren, that flesh and blood cannot inherit the kingdom of God; neither doth corruption inherit incorruption.** 51 Behold, I shew you a mystery; We shall not all sleep,

but <u>we shall all be changed</u>, *52* In a moment, in the twinkling of an eye, at the last trump: for the trumpet shall sound, **and the dead shall be raised incorruptible, and <u>we shall be changed.</u>** *53* <u>For this corruptible **must** put on incorruption,</u> and this mortal must put on immortality."

As you can see in the scripture above, you do not get to take your current body that has blood in it into heaven; it cannot live in heaven because it is subject to decay. **In other words, our current bodies cannot survive in heaven because they are corruptible or biodegradable.** The type of body that lives in heaven cannot have blood flowing through it. It is why the scripture above says that we (our bodies) <u>shall be changed</u> in the twinkling of an eye before rapture.

This is also why at the end, our bodies will be glorified to be like celestial bodies that can live in heaven and can live on earth; which can pass through walls and are not be limited by space, time, and earthly objects or material things. This way, we can flow between heaven and earth as God's children and as His representative government on the new earth. Our new bodies will enable us to do this just as the Lord Jesus can move between heaven and earth now. Today, He can eat on earth without a need to eliminate waste and His body is no longer subject to the elements on earth. It defies gravity and all of the other limitations that our bodies are currently subjected to.

I want you to know that only those who are <u>born again</u> have the promise of receiving such bodies because the Lord Jesus said that if you are born of flesh, you are going to remain flesh but when you are born of the **Holy Spirit**, you are going to become a spirit being that is connected forever with God **(John 3:6)**. Know therefore that since you are born again, you are not just a spirit being living in a body having a soul but you are connected spiritually and divinely with your **Creator** forever! In other words, the **Holy Spirit** connects us with God through His Son, Jesus Christ. This is why the Lord Jesus can look at us today and say in **John 17:20-23** that we are one with Him just as He is one with the Father by the **Holy Spirit:**

> "Neither pray I for these alone, but for them also which shall believe on me through their word; 21 **That they all may be one; as thou, <u>Father, art in me</u>, and <u>I in thee</u>, that they also <u>may be one in us</u>: that the world may believe that thou hast sent me.** 22 And the glory which thou gavest me I have given them; **that they may be one, even as we are one:** 23 <u>**I in them**</u>, and **<u>thou in me</u>**, that **<u>they may be made perfect in one</u>**…"

The Holy Spirit Helps Us to Worship God in Spirit

We are told in **John 4:23-24** that God is a Spirit and those that worship Him must worship Him in spirit and in truth. You can only worship God in spirit and in truth when you are born of His Spirit or when you are <u>born again</u>; connected to Him spirit (your human spirit) to Spirit (Holy Spirit):

> "<u>But the hour cometh, and now is, when the true worshippers shall worship the Father in spirit and in truth</u>: for the Father seeketh such to worship him. 24 **God is a Spirit: and they that worship him must worship him in <u>spirit and in truth</u>.**"

It is impossible to worship **God the Father** in spirit when you do not have His Spirit — the **Holy Spirit** dwelling in your human spirit. When you become filled with the **Holy Spirit**, you receive the gift of tongues that enables you to speak mysteries to God in the heavenly language:

> "**For he that speaketh in an unknown tongue speaketh not unto men, but unto God:** for no man understandeth him; **howbeit in the spirit he speaketh mysteries**" (1 Corinthians 14:2).

Chapter 5
The Holy Spirit is the Gift of God to all Believers

The Holy Spirit as a Gift

In this chapter, we are going to examine the **Holy Spirit as the gift of God to all believers** and how that He is **transferable**. The **Holy Spirit** is the gift that God promised to every single person who believes in the Lord Jesus Christ. This why the Apostle Peter said the following in **Acts 2:37-39:**

> "Now when they heard this, they were pricked in their heart, and said unto Peter and to the rest of the apostles, Men and brethren, what shall we do? *38* Then Peter said unto them, **Repent, and be baptized every one of you in the name of Jesus Christ for the remission of sins, and ye shall receive the gift of the Holy Ghost.** *39* For the **promise** is unto you, and to your children, and to all that are afar off, even as many as the Lord our God shall call."

The scriptures also record the following in **Acts 10:45** concerning the Gentiles who believed in the Lord after hearing Peter's words about Him:

> "And they of the circumcision which believed were astonished, as many as came with Peter, **because that on the Gentiles also was poured out the gift of the Holy Ghost.**"

In **Romans 1:10-11**, we see the **Holy Spirit** referred to as the **spiritual gift**. In this scripture, the Apostle Paul is talking about the churches that were under him and how he has been praying for them and making requests on their behalf to God that He may send him to them so that they can receive the **Holy Spirit:**

"Making request, if by any means now at length I might have a prosperous journey by the will of God to come unto you. *11* **For I long to see you, that I may impart unto you <u>some spiritual gift</u>, to the end ye may be established.**"

As you can see in the scripture above, the Apostle Paul did not say some spiritual **gifts** because the **Holy Spirit** is the major gift that God gives to the believers. Once you receive the **Holy Spirit**, He then helps you to receive all the other gifts that God has for you in Christ. It is why the Apostle Paul desired so much to see the believers in Rome so that he could impart (release) the **Holy Spirit** to them. We are now going to look at how the **Holy Spirit** is given from one person to another. It is a process called impartation or transference.

Transferring the Holy Spirit through Laying on of Hands

To transfer or impart something from one person to another means to, **"to grant, to share, to transmit, to remove or to convey from one place or person to another."** Remember what the Lord Jesus said in **Matthew 19:26** that, *"With God, all things are possible?"* **Yes, God is able to transfer Himself in the Person of His Spirit from one person to another!** This is why we can safely say that the **Lord Holy Spirit** is transferable. **Because the Holy Spirit is transferable, He can be made <u>a</u> gift to new** believers by the laying on of hands or by asking through the spoken words.

Before my salvation experience, I was totally ignorant about the <u>laying on of hands to receive the **Holy Spirit**</u>. As a matter of fact, I was very resistant to the things of God and to being born again. When my mother stressed the need for me to be born again, I thought that she was trying to recruit me to join her church and I refused. I looked at my mother and youngest sister as two fanatics who took the Bible way too far and I did not want anything to do with what they were doing.

I did not want to change churches because <u>I had been taught</u> that the denomination that I was a part of at the time was the "true church that was started by the Apostle Peter." Therefore, to me, it was a case of why seek the lesser when you have the greater; Peter was the elder and leader of the Church after the **Lord Jesus** went back to heaven. With this mindset, I viewed the whole born again teaching as a new found doctrine from newer churches and I resisted it.

Besides, I thought I knew so much and that I could debate anyone that brought up the subject of religion. **Something in me changed when I allowed a spirit-filled Christian to hold my hands and pray for me. Without knowing it, I had an encounter with the Anointing** and I wrote about it in one of my books titled, ***How to Discern and Expel Evil Spirits.*** Here is the excerpt from *Chapter 1*, pages 33-37:

> *"Example of How Evil Spirits*
> *Tried to Prevent My Salvation:*
> *For years, nobody could preach the Gospel to me to get me saved. It did not matter what you said, I had a counter argument because God gave me a very bright mind. There was no way you were going to tell me a spiritual truth or occurrence that I did not have a logical explanation for. So, for many years, I could not get saved. But one day, I was sitting in church with my mom, and she got really sad because here she was in this ministry and in leadership but she has a daughter that cares nothing about what goes on in the church. I was just there to get her off my back. On this day, one of the ushers came up to me and said, 'Don't you think it's about time you gave your life to Christ?' And I said, 'Is it by force?' And he said 'No.' I said, 'OK, so get off my back.' I then turned around and looked at my mom and it looked like she had lost everything that was valuable in*

life. She was looking very miserable so I answered the alter call but the Pastor did not pray for us to get saved. I want to say to all Pastors, please, pray for the people while you have them. Do not send them to some other place because you might lose some of them. They almost lost me in this process and this is how it happened.

We were taken out of the sanctuary into another room. When I got into the room, I was assigned to a lady to talk to me. At this time, I did not know that I was demon possessed but I was well dressed and I was looking good! The lady I was assigned to said to me, 'Oh, after I finish praying for you, you're going to become a saint.' You never say that to a Roman Catholic person because the way we were taught about becoming a saint when I was a Catholic is that for you to be a saint, you have to have lived and died. After 200 years, the Pope tells them to dig up your bones and they will then pronounce you a saint after examining all your good deeds.

To my knowledge, that was how they made saints. Therefore, I found it absurd for the lady to tell me that she was going to make me a saint! I looked at her and said: 'You make me a saint; You?' She said, 'yes.' (God is really laughing now because He remembers that incident!) I said, 'I am sorry, I am sorry for you and I am sorry for whoever has been putting those ideas in your head that you can make someone a saint, but I think I'm in the wrong place!' So I turned around and was about to walk off and she said, 'You're not going to pray to receive salvation?' And I said, 'Not if you're going to make me a saint!' She asked me again, 'You're leaving?' And I said, 'Watch me!'

I could still see this lady and her desperation to get through to me on that day that I needed to get saved. She did not want to grab me because it would appear too forceful. She did not know how to get it into my 'demon-laden head' at that time that I needed salvation; that I was barely making it. *Not knowing what else to do, she ran after me as I was about to leave the room and I looked at her and I saw that she was very concerned about me as though I was going to drop dead the next minute.* **She said to me, 'Well, since you don't want to get saved, can I pray for you?' And I said, 'Of course'.** *Roman Catholics always go to get prayed for so I did not mind her praying for me as long as she did not try to make me a saint.* **She took my hands and she prayed for me.**

When I got back into the sanctuary, my mom asked me, 'Did you get saved?' I said, No, because the lady did not know how to make a saint. Why would I let somebody who is ignorant about how someone becomes a saint get me saved.' She said, 'You didn't get saved?' And I said, 'No'. <u>This happened at the Sunday service.</u> <u>Do you know that the Tuesday of that week I got saved?</u>

At this particular time as I stated in my book, **Unveiling the God-Mother,** *I was about to come back to the United States and my mom said, 'Go say goodbye to the Pastor.' I was glad because I had wanted to talk to the Pastor about taking 10% tithes from my mom. I had an issue with that and I wanted to tell him to lay off my mom's 10%. Therefore, I was very glad at the opportunity to set him straight. So I went to the meeting all armed to fight this Pastor.* **When he opened the door, I heard a voice say, 'peace be still.'** *Whatever rage I came in with just went away and he began to talk to me. For the first time in my life, somebody was making sense with something that had to do with the Bible or with religion and I sat there and listened. I got saved at this meeting with the Pastor just two days after my encounter with the lady. The Lord said to me years later:*

*'***Do you know what happened to you? Those demons had their fingers plugged into your ears. Nothing**

anybody said to you could get in but <u>when you</u> *<u>allowed that spirit-filled lady to touch you, you</u>* *<u>made contact with the Holy Spirit and the demons</u>* *<u>fled</u>.' That lady was the first spirit-filled person that I* *ever truly and willingly made contact with and received a* *blessing from. It was just a brief encounter and a blessing* *but I received it.*

I said all that to tell you that just in line with the *handkerchiefs taken from Paul's body, when you a* *spirit-filled person makes contact with <u>unbelievers</u>,* *it does good things for them; not just brushing against* *someone because I was living in the same house with my* *mom, but I was not receiving what she had to say. But* *this other lady, I received the blessing she prayed over me.* *According to the Lord, when I willingly made that* *contact with her, the demons fled and I got saved* *two days later. She was critical to my salvation, because* *without her, I would not have received the Gospel and* *become saved."*

My salvation experience was the working of the **Holy Spirit**. As you saw, it began with a spirit-filled lady who made a spiritual contact with me and the contact drove away the evil spirits that were responsible for making me to debate people who had tried to share the Gospel of Jesus Christ with me. **When I finally got saved, the Pastor laid his hands on me to receive the Holy Spirit;** it takes the **Holy Spirit** for somebody to get saved. As you saw from my experience, the **Holy Spirit** can be given or transferred from a believer to a new believer through bodily contact such as laying on of hands. Laying on of hands is one of the doctrines of the Church of Jesus Christ as we see in **Hebrews 6:2:**

> "Of the doctrine of baptisms, and of **laying on** **of hands**, and of resurrection of the dead, and of eternal judgment."

He is the Seal on all Believers

The Apostle Paul informed us in **Ephesians 1:13-14** about the Lord's promise of sending the **Holy Spirit** to seal us as we become the Lord's purchased possessions:

> "In whom ye also trusted, after that ye heard the word of truth, the gospel of your salvation: in whom also after that ye believed, **ye were sealed with that holy Spirit of promise,** *14* **Which is the earnest of our inheritance until the redemption of the purchased possession,** unto the praise of his glory."

Once we receive the **Holy Spirit**, God uses Him to seal us so that when evil spirits come against us without us giving them permission by making an evil covenant with them, the **Holy Spirit** rises up inside of us to defend us.

Also, when the devil sends an evil assignment against us with any of his evil spirits, it the **Holy Spirit** that uses the Word of God that we speak to drive away the evil spirits. He will also drive away evil spirits that we have already registered our distaste for in our spiritual desires. For example, when I first started to minister to people, the Lord informed me that if I was going to be a successful Christian minister here in the United States, I needed to overcome specific spirits. One of them was the spirit of obesity/gluttony because it is an assignment that the devil has sent against people that live in this country. He then gave me a vision of how the spirit operates and how the **Holy Spirit** drove it away from me. It was an open vision and it was very, very interesting how He did it:

How the Holy Spirit Drove Away the Spirit of Obesity/Gluttony from Me

In the physical, I was lying in bed in my bedroom and I saw a vision of me in the kitchen sitting on a chair and this really huge and extremely obese lady (a spirit) came into the kitchen. She was mean-looking and she spread her legs as she began to try to sit on me. As I watched her, I began to scream in my bedroom, "NO, Lord Jesus..." but she proceeded to sit on me anyway. As I watched her, I could see that she was determined to totally absorb herself into me so I continued to call on the Lord.

*<u>As she sat on me thinking that she had successfully taken over my body and she positioned herself to really begin to expand and absorb herself into me,</u> **I saw the hand of the Holy Spirit reach out from inside of me. He pinched her buttocks and she jumped up screaming as she fled.** I mean, she was up, off of me, and out of the kitchen very quickly. She fled through the window and I said to her, "Serves you right for trying to sit on me and expand yourself into me in your attempt to make me fat." From the shock that was on her face as she fled, I could tell that she was not prepared for what she encountered from the **Holy Spirit** that dwells in me. I praise God for His awesome power. I saw the power of Him that dwells in me because I believe in Christ.*

According to the Lord, when she is <u>able to successfully</u> sit on someone, she takes away the ability of the person to feel full after eating because she keeps expanding the person to desire more and more food. As a result, the person continues to require more and more food because the person cannot feel full even after eating a large meal. That is why Christians who are battling obesity or have a weight problem need the help of the **Holy Spirit. From what I saw, the spirit of obesity is no match for the Holy Spirit and not just the obesity spirit but all evil spirits.** You should therefore, connect with the Lord **Holy Spirit** by receiving Christ as your Lord and Savior.

When you tap into the power of the **Holy Spirit** and you say, "No" to an evil assignment, He will help you to overcome the evil assignment and the evil spirit behind it. In my case, I was not aware that an assignment had been sent against me to make me obese but the **Lord Holy Spirit** knew and He was ready and waiting to dislodge her from me and He wanted me to see it. Praise the Lord!

A Word to Christians Battling Obesity

I want to share something with Christians who are battling this spirit of obesity in their lives. If you remember, I said that the Lord told me that in order to be a successful minister in the United States, I needed to overcome certain spirits and one of the spirits is the spirit of obesity. **The reason is because the obesity spirit is a principality.** In other words, she is sent by the devil against this nation; against those who live here. One of the reasons that many Christians have not been successful in getting rid of her in their lives is because they tend to war against her on the level of "spiritual wickedness" instead of the "principality" level.

Because she is a principality, you have to deal with her on that level. **Principalities** are sent against nations and **spiritual wickedness** is the lowest level of spiritual warfare there is. Fighting at the "spiritual wickedness" level means, warring against the general wickedness that you can see or perceive around you; be it with people, places or things. You must also fight the evil spiritual assignments against you from the level of **evil principalities that control those who have power** in nations, states or local governments. The **rulers of darkness** represent the demonic and occult realm. Ephesians 6 will help me to clarify this point to you because it outlines the different levels at which we wage spiritual warfare. Be sure to pray according to **Ephesians 6:11-12:**

> "Put on the whole armour of God, that ye may be able to stand against the wiles of the devil. 12 For we wrestle not against flesh and blood, but

against principalities, against powers, against the rulers of the darkness of this world, against **spiritual wickedness in high places."**

It pays to know how the evil spirits war against us; for instance, the spirit of obesity especially likes to go after every single person that loves the Lord because she wants to weight them down with being over-weight physically so that they cannot go about doing the things of the Lord. Her strategy is not only to slow you down but to spoil your self-image and your self-esteem so that you are <u>too self-conscious</u> to do the things that you would like to do; including stepping out to serve the Lord. She is a very wicked spirit.

Therefore, in this nation, she is after your energy, your health, your money, your image and your time. She wants you to spend a large portion of your income on trying to fight her (doctors' bills and other healthcare costs) so that you do not have much left for other things. As a result, the medical, pharmaceutical, diet and exercise industries rake in billions of dollars each year. **You can see why she targets this nation because we have many people who if unencumbered by obesity, will go out and do great things for the Lord.**

Chapter 6
The Holy Spirit is the Spirit of Prophecy

What is Prophecy?
The following are some of the general **definitions** of **Prophecy**:

1. An inspired utterance of God's prophet that is viewed as a revelation of divine will.
2. A prediction of the future that is made under divine inspiration.
3. A divinely inspired message or prediction transmitted orally or in writing.
4. The vocational duty of a prophet.

In our case or in Christianity, **prophecy means utterances by spirit-filled Christians or utterances under the inspiration of the Holy Spirit**. If you are <u>born again</u> and <u>can pray</u>, you <u>can also prophesy</u> because we are told in **Revelation 19:10** that the **testimony of Jesus is the <u>Spirit of Prophecy</u>.** It is the **Holy Spirit** that helps us to prophesy; it is not something that you should do by yourself because true prophecy comes to pass**:**

> "...**For the testimony of Jesus is the spirit of prophecy.**"

What this also means is that when we are born again, the **Holy Spirit** begins to help us testify about the Lord Jesus. This is one of the reasons that He came as we can clearly see in **1 Corinthians 12:3** because without the help of the **Holy Spirit**, no man can even say that Jesus is Lord. In other words, no man or woman can **come to Christ** without the **Holy Spirit:**

> "<u>Wherefore I give you to understand, that no man speaking by the Spirit of God calleth Jesus accursed</u>: **and that no man can say that Jesus is the Lord, <u>but</u> by the Holy Ghost.**"

Not only do we need the **Holy Spirit** to help us confess Jesus as Lord, we also need Him to help us bear testimony of the works of Christ to unbelievers so that they can be born again or saved. Therefore, it is the **Holy Spirit** that helps us declare why the Lord Jesus came into the earth, what He did for humanity on the Cross and in the grave, the meaning of His death and resurrection and what He did with His blood when He went back into heaven. **He helps us to minister the Gospel with the demonstration of His power and His wisdom.**

Why Do We Need Prophecy?

The scriptures tell us in **1 Corinthians 14:1-31** that the purpose of personal prophecy is **to edify, to exhort** and **to comfort** believers in the Church and to minister to unbelievers. The **Holy Spirit** is the one who helps us to accomplish these things:

> "Follow after charity, and desire spiritual gifts, **but rather that ye may prophesy**. 2 For he that speaketh in an unknown tongue speaketh not unto men, but unto God: for no man understandeth him; howbeit in the spirit he speaketh mysteries. 3 **But he that prophesieth speaketh unto men to edification**, and **exhortation**, and **comfort**. 4 He that speaketh in an unknown tongue edifieth himself; **but he that prophesieth edifieth the church...**

> 23 If therefore the whole church be come together into one place, and all speak with tongues, and there come in those that are unlearned, or unbelievers, will they not say that ye are mad? 24 **But if all prophesy, and there come in one that believeth not, or one unlearned, he is convinced of all, he is judged of all:**

25 And thus are the secrets of his heart made manifest; and so falling down on his face he will worship God, and report that God is in you of a truth. 26 How is it then, brethren? when ye come together, every one of you hath a <u>psalm</u>, hath a <u>doctrine</u>, hath a <u>tongue</u>, hath a <u>revelation</u>, hath an <u>interpretation</u>. **Let all things be done unto <u>edifying</u>...** 31 <u>**For ye may all prophesy one by one**</u>, **that all may learn, and <u>all may be comforted</u>.**"

While ministering to believers and unbelievers, the **Holy Spirit** gives us prophetic utterances – prophecy. This is one of the reasons why we can say things to people; things that only God knows about them to their surprise. We can even make prediction about future events to them under the inspiration of the **Holy Spirit**. Having said that, I immediately want to draw your attention to the fact that there are many voices in the earth realm today; from Nostradamus to the psychic around the corner that claim to speak prophecy but we know that any utterance or prediction outside of the **Holy Spirit** is demonic and is not to be received.

Prophecy is by the Will of the Holy Spirit

Prophecy is at the discretion of the **Holy Spirit**. What this means is that you cannot truly prophesy without Him or without His leading as we see in **2 Peter 1:21:**

> "<u>For the prophecy came not in old time by the will of man</u>: **but holy men of God spake as they were moved by the Holy Ghost.**"

The key point to remember is that <u>the **Holy Spirit** moves us based on the proportion of our faith at the time of speaking</u>. Some people have **great or strong faith**; some people have **little faith** while others have **no faith** at all. Therefore, we cannot just open our mouths and speak when the **Holy Spirit** is not moving us to. **Also, we cannot speak things that we have no faith to believe God for (either for us or for other people) because the accuracy of our prophecy is directly related to the level of our faith.** This is why the Apostle Paul issued the following admonition in **Romans 12:6:**

> "Having then <u>gifts differing according to the grace that is given to us</u>, whether prophecy, **let us prophesy according to the proportion of faith** 7 Or ministry, let us wait on our ministering: or he that teacheth, on teaching..."

You should not prophesy grandiose things that you cannot exercise your faith to truly believe God for just to impress people. Most of us have heard "prophets" giving some very "lofty and fluffy prophetic words" in order to get people to give them money but because God is not in these words and their faith does not match the level at which they prophesy, their words do not come to pass. Therefore, learn to prophesy at the level of your faith but know that you are to grow in faith.

In my personal experience, there had been times when I was giving someone a word and wanted to stop because I thought that the word was promising or giving the person way too much and the Lord would tell me, "Do not stop; it is me, continue." **He then began to teach me that there comes a time when our mind and His mind become one — the mind of Christ.** As I said before, your accuracy will increase as your faith and trust in the Lord's abilities increase. He wants to flow through you uninterrupted by fear, doubt or unbelief.

For example, when you first began to prophesy, you were very conscious and afraid of making mistakes or prophesying something that God has not said. As a result, your mind was in the way of the **Holy Spirit** when it comes to prophesying because you were looking to yourself for accuracy rather than placing your trust in Him. As you learned to relax and believe the Lord's words in **Matthew 10:20** that, *"it is the Spirit of your father that speaketh in you,"* the **Holy Spirit** began to have more freedom to move or flow through you. As your faith in Him grew, so did your accuracy:

> **"For it is not ye that speak,** <u>but the **Spirit of your Father** </u>**which speaketh in you."**

The Holy Spirit on Old Testament Prophets

The **Holy Spirit** moved in both the Old and New Testament prophets, and on holy men and women of God. In the **Old Testament**, the **Holy Spirit** in most cases would <u>rest upon the head of a prophet</u> and the prophet would begin to prophesy as we see in **2 Chronicles 24:20:**

> **"And the Spirit of God came upon Zechariah the son of Jehoiada the priest, which stood above the people, and said unto them, Thus saith God,** Why transgress ye the commandments of the LORD, that ye cannot prosper? because ye have forsaken the LORD, he hath also forsaken you."

Sometimes, the Holy Spirit was also the unction on the <u>scribes</u> and they would write the Word of the Lord under His inspiration. In the case of John the Baptist and his parents, they were **all** filled with the **Holy Spirit**. According to **Luke 1:41:44**, John the Baptist was filled with the **Holy Spirit** while he was still in his mother's womb:

> "And it came to pass, that, when Elisabeth heard the salutation of Mary, the babe leaped in her womb; and Elisabeth was filled with the Holy Ghost: 42 And she spake out with a loud voice,

and said, Blessed art thou among women, and blessed is the fruit of thy womb. *43* And whence is this to me, that the mother of my Lord should come to me? *44* **For, lo, as soon as the voice of thy salutation sounded in mine ears, the babe leaped in my womb for joy.**"

And **Luke 1:67-72:**

"**And his father Zacharias was filled with the Holy Ghost, and prophesied,** saying, *68* Blessed be the Lord God of Israel; for he hath visited and redeemed his people, *69* And hath raised up an horn of salvation for us in the house of his servant David; *70* As he spake by the mouth of his holy prophets, which have been since the world began: *71* That we should be saved from our enemies, and from the hand of all that hate us; *72* To perform the mercy promised to our fathers, and to remember his holy covenant…"

As for the **New Testament** believers, we already saw in Acts 2:1-4 that the **Holy Spirit** rested upon the heads of the New Testament believers and filled them up at the same time. Also, after the Lord Jesus rose from the dead, He breathed the **Holy Spirit** on the disciples. As a result, we can safely say that the **Holy Spirit** can rest on the head of the New Testament believers, He can fill the believers, and as unction, He can move in the believers.

Chapter 7
The Gifts of the Holy Spirit

The Nine Gifts of the Holy Spirit

When the **Holy Spirit** comes into the life of a Christian to take up residence, He actually comes with what we call the nine gifts of the Spirit. These gifts are outlined in **1 Corinthians 12:7-11:**

> "But the manifestation of the Spirit is given to every man to profit withal. *8* For to one is given by the Spirit *(the Holy Spirit)* the **word of wisdom** *(knowledge about future things or events);* to another **the word of knowledge** *(knowledge about past or present things or events)* by the same Spirit; *9* another **faith** by the same Spirit; to another the **gifts of healing** by the same Spirit;
>
> *10* To another the **working of miracles;** to another **prophecy;** to another **discerning of spirits;** to another **divers kinds of tongues;** to another the **interpretation of tongues:** *11* <u>**But all these worketh that one and the selfsame Spirit, dividing to every man severally as he will**</u>."

These gifts endue you with all the abilities that you will need to be able to do whatever God requires you to do. **When you receive the baptism of the Holy Spirit, believe it or not; you can raise the dead, you can cast out devils, you can speak in tongues and you can do everything that your mind tells you that you cannot do.** The only thing is that you have to be led by the **Holy Spirit.** For example, if you are in a place and someone suddenly drops dead and the **Holy Spirit** says to you; go over there and lay hands on that corpse and you obey, that person will rise up from the dead. It is not by your might or by your power but by the power of the **Holy Spirit.**

The Lord has been showing me that doing miracles, signs and wonders is really just following His instructions. In other words, operating in the gifts of the **Holy Spirit** means following the instructions you receive from Him without fear or doubt. He illustrated this point to me by giving me the example of when Saul (before he became the Apostle Paul) was struck blind on the road to Damascus and how the disciple named Ananias followed His instructions that resulted in Saul receiving his sight —a miracle! When you read the story in **Acts 9:8-19**, you will see that Ananias was very reluctant about going to Saul's house but he had faith in the Lord's ability and he obeyed the Lord's instruction:

> "And Saul arose from the earth; and when his eyes were opened, he saw no man: but they led him by the hand, and brought him into Damascus. *9* And he was three days without sight, and neither did eat nor drink. *10* <u>And there was a certain disciple at Damascus, named Ananias; and to him said the Lord in a vision, Ananias. And he said, Behold, I am here, Lord. *11* And the Lord said unto him, Arise, and go into the street which is called Straight, and enquire in the house of Judas for one called Saul, of Tarsus: for, behold, he prayeth,</u>
>
> *12* <u>And hath seen in a vision a man named Ananias coming in, and putting his hand on him, that he might receive his sight.</u> 13 **Then Ananias answered, Lord, I have heard by many of this man, how much evil he hath done to thy saints at Jerusalem: 14 And here he hath authority from the chief priests to bind all that call on thy name.** 15 <u>But the Lord said unto him, Go thy way: for he is a chosen vessel unto me, to bear my name before the Gentiles, and kings, and the children of Israel</u>: *16* For I will shew him how great things he must suffer for my name's sake.

17 **And Ananias went his way, and entered into the house; and putting his hands on him said, Brother Saul, the Lord, even Jesus, that appeared unto thee in the way as thou camest, hath sent me, that thou mightest receive thy sight, and be filled with the Holy Ghost.** 18 <u>And immediately there fell from his eyes as it had been scales: and he received sight forthwith, and arose, and was baptized.</u> 19 And when he had received meat, he was strengthened..."

As you can see, Ananias went to Saul's house reluctantly but the Lord used him because he had faith and was obedient. Although he was not enthusiastic about going to meet Saul, he obeyed the Lord's instruction to go. Look at what he said to Saul, *"Brother Saul, the Lord, even Jesus, that appeared unto thee in the way as thou camest, hath sent me, that thou mightest receive thy sight, and be filled with the Holy Ghost."* He did not say, "I come in the name of the Lord Jesus; be healed."

The reason is because Ananias did not make the assignment personal; he went purely in obedience to the Lord and he just laid his hands on Saul and Saul received his sight. He did not personally care for Saul and as a matter of fact, he was afraid of Saul because Saul was a well known persecutor of Christians. Therefore, sending him to Saul was like sending someone into a lion's den. What this proves is that obedience matters a lot in the Kingdom of God so, when you get instructions from the **Holy Spirit** and you obey, He gives you the instant breakthrough, the miracles and the signs and wonders that you are looking for. We have to cultivate obedience to the **Holy Spirit**.

When the **Holy Spirit** comes into our lives, He endues us with everything that we need so that anytime God calls on us to do something, we are more than able to do it because of the power of the **Holy Spirit** that flows in and through us. Again, we all have the ability to raise the dead, heal the sick, cast out devils, etc. When the Lord Jesus gave the commandment in **Mark 16:15-18** to, **"Go ye"** into all the world and preach the Gospel and to raise the dead, to cast out devils, and to cleanse the lepers, we all know that He was not just speaking to **"brother Ye"** in China. We are all the **"Ye"** that He commanded to go:

> "And he said unto them, **Go ye** *(all of us)* **into all the world, and preach the gospel to every creature.** *16* He that believeth and is baptized shall be saved; but he that believeth not shall be damned. *17* **And these signs shall follow them that believe; In my name shall they cast out devils; they shall speak with new tongues;** *18* **They shall take up serpents; and if they drink any deadly thing, it shall not hurt them; they shall lay hands on the sick, and they shall recover**."

Yes, we can all fulfill this great commission from the Lord in the above scripture by the power of the **Holy Spirit** that dwells in us. The key is obedience to His instructions.

Administration of the Gifts by the Holy Spirit

We have seen in the paragraphs above that as prophetic people, we all receive the <u>fullness</u> of the **Holy Spirit** and we all have the ability to manifest His gifts but He operates in and though us <u>differently</u>. In general, it means that whenever you need to manifest a particular aspect of the **gift of the Holy Spirit**, you have the ability to do it by the power of the **Holy Spirit** that is in you and with you. For example, when you <u>have met His requirement</u> and you need a **word of wisdom**, the **Holy Spirit** will move upon you and you can get a **word of wisdom** from Him.

At another time, you might need a **word of knowledge** and He will give it to you at that time. It might be faith, healing, miracle, prophecy, interpretation of tongues, discerning of spirits, etc., that you need and the **Holy Spirit** will give them to you because He divides to every "man severally as He will." **His will as your helper is to give you what you need when you need it but you have to meet His required standard.**

What I am saying here is that just because the Holy Spirit has given you the gifts and the ability to demonstrate them does not mean that you will manifest them if you do not meet God's criteria for manifesting them. We have to have this balanced understanding of how the **Holy Spirit** administers the gifts because it also does not mean that just because you have the **Holy Spirit and His gifts,** the stars and the moon are going to flicker everywhere you go and that you can at your own will begin to manifest the gifts without His administration.

We will do well to always remember that it is the Holy Spirit that checks out the situation and determines the gifts that those who meet His criteria can flow in to help them accomplish God's will concerning any given circumstance. Just think about it: How many of you have prayed for someone and they recover or prayed for someone and nothing happened? How many of you have prophesied over someone and the words came to pass or prophesied to someone and nothing happened? The reason is because **receiving the gift and manifesting the gifts are two different things.** Manifesting the gifts is also the administration of the **Holy Spirit** who gave the gifts. Therefore, as a believer, you have God's abilities in you because of who dwells inside of you but demonstrating the ability requires that you fulfill God's righteous requirements.

To reiterate the importance of the **Holy Spirit** in the life of the believer, I want everyone who reads this book to know that <u>only when the</u> **Holy Spirit** <u>comes into our lives</u> <u>as believers in the Lord Jesus Christ do we receive and begin</u> <u>to display the</u> **nine gifts of the Holy Spirit** <u>because,</u> **He is** **the one that gives and activates the gifts.** Unfortunately, **there are several denominational churches that teach their** **members to reject the works of the Holy Spirit and His gifts.** As a result, these denominations do not manifest the **gifts of** **the Holy Spirit** and they do not interact with the **Godhead** in their daily Christian walk. **They are living below the level** **of spiritual capacity that God Almighty has called them to.** They are living according to **2 Timothy 3:5:**

> "Having a form of godliness, **but denying the** **power thereof**: from such turn away."

Again, always remember that it is one thing to receive the **gifts of the Holy Spirit** as a prophetic person but it is another thing to have the gifts actually flow through you when you minister. <u>God is faithful to give us all the gifts</u> but releasing the gifts through us during our ministering is another thing. We will now look at how God chooses <u>whom to release the</u> <u>gifts through</u>.

The Fairness of the Holy Spirit Concerning the Gifts

We are not to be ignorant about how the **Holy Spirit** <u>administers His gifts</u> and we saw the **nine gifts of the Holy** **Spirit** but now, we are going to take a look at how these gifts are <u>administered</u> by the **Holy Spirit**. To do this, we need to take a second look at **1 Corinthians 12:4-11.** What you will see right away are the <u>three titles</u> of the **Holy Spirit**. He is **Lord**, He is **God** and He is **Spirit** because He is part of the **Godhead**. He is not independent from **God the Father** and **God the Son** (Jesus); they are one and they work as one. Therefore, He is righteous and He is fair; very fair concerning the gifts and all other things:

"Now there are **diversities of gifts**, but the same Spirit. *5* And there are **differences of administrations**, but the **same Lord**. *6* And there are **diversities of operations**, but it is the **same God** which worketh all in all. *7* But the manifestation of the Spirit is given to every man to profit withal. *8* **For to one is given by the Spirit** the **word of wisdom**; to another the **word of knowledge by the same Spirit**;

9 To another **faith by the same Spirit**; to another the **gifts of healing by the same Spirit**; *10* To another the **working of miracles**; to another **prophecy**; to another **discerning of spirits**; to another **divers kinds of tongues**; to another the **interpretation of tongues**: *11* But **all these worketh that one and the selfsame Spirit, dividing to every man severally as he will.**"

We know that God does not play favorites so; how does the **Holy Spirit** determine who manifests what? In other words, as the **administrator** of the **nine gifts**, how does the **Holy Spirit** determined who can manifest certain gifts at any given time? **What are the righteous requirements or criteria that God is looking for?** The answers are found in the Lord's Jesus' parable in **Matthew 25:14-15:**

"For the kingdom of heaven is as a man travelling into a far country, who called his own servants, and delivered unto them his goods. *15* And unto one he gave five talents, to another two, and to another one; **to every man according to his several ability;** and straightway took his journey."

What we learn from this parable is that the manifestation of the gifts of God upon our lives is according to the abilities

(seriousness) **that He sees us already <u>willing to display or manifest concerning His call upon our lives</u>.** With God, there always has to be first; **a willingness on our part.** For example, God can call you to do some mighty works for Him and you can choose to ignore it. As a result, the **Holy Spirit** will not require the manifestation of His gifts through you. Some people do not spend time with God in prayer or in His Word and God will not require His gifts to be manifested through them also. You have those who wait until there is a crisis and then begin to pray fearful (faithless) prayers for God's intervention and they wonder why God does not answer them.

Also, in Christendom, we have people who talk a good Christian talk but when God looks at them, they do not walk-the-walk. There are others who pay Him lip-service on Sundays and in their lives. **To God, you must not only be willing to live by every Word that came out of His mouth, but you must be a faithful and obedient servant to manifest His gifts.** I remember a time when He asked me the following question: *"Would you delegate someone to go and represent you when you know that the person will not <u>faithfully</u> represent you?"* My reply was, *"No"* and He said, "Neither will I."

Therefore, we all stand to learn about His administration of the gifts by what He said concerning King David in **Acts 13:22:**

> "And when he had removed him *(King Saul)*, he raised up unto them David to be their king; to whom also he gave testimony, and said, **I have found David the son of Jesse, <u>a man after mine own heart</u>, which shall <u>fulfill all my will</u>.**"

We must learn to pursue God and to serve Him with all our hearts, all our minds, all our souls and all our bodies and we must be faithful to live according to His will. When you do this, you will see God release His gifts through you. He is actually looking for faithful servants through whom He can release the gifts:

> **"For the eyes of the LORD run to and fro throughout the whole earth, to shew himself strong in the behalf of them whose heart is perfect toward him..."** (2 Chronicles 16:9).

And also in **Proverbs 20:6:**

> "Most men will proclaim everyone his own goodness: **but a faithful man who can find?"**

We have people who occupy certain offices that require the manifestation of the gifts of the **Holy Spirit** on a constant basis. Some of those people are prophets. Therefore, we need to look at the Office of the Prophet.

The Office of the Prophet

As you have just seen, God does not play favorites; **He merely releases through each and every one of us, the gifts He sees us willing to pay the price to see manifest in our lives.** Apart from moving in the <u>occasional flow of prophetic gifts</u> such as **words of wisdom, words of knowledge**, healing, discerning of spirits, etc., there are those in the body of Christ who occupy the <u>Office of the Prophet</u> and **the Holy Spirit will anoint them according to the requirement of the office.** For example, those who are **Prophets** need to <u>flow constantly in gifts</u> such as **word of knowledge, word of wisdom, prophecy, discerning of spirits, understanding dreams and visions,** etc., while those who do not occupy the office will have the <u>occasional flow</u> of the gifts.

The reason for this is because people and nations constantly look to Prophets to help them understand the

things of the Lord. <u>They have to be able to see into the</u> <u>spiritual realm and to interpret the mind of God concerning</u> <u>people's everyday life and problems.</u> A case in point is the circumstances of how Saul became the first king in Israel. He went to see the Prophet Samuel in order <u>to learn about the</u> <u>fate of his father's missing sheep.</u> When he met the Prophet Samuel, not only did he learn about the fate of the sheep, he also found out that God had chosen him to be Israel's first king —**1 Samuel 9:3-21:**

"And Kish said to <u>Saul</u> his son, Take now one of the servants with thee, and arise, **go seek the asses**. 4 And he passed through mount Ephraim, and passed through the land of Shalisha, **but they found them not...** 5 Saul said to his servant that was with him, <u>Come, and let us return; lest</u> <u>my father leave caring for the asses, and take</u> <u>thought for us.</u> 6 And he said unto him, <u>Behold</u> <u>now, there is in this city a man of God, and he</u> <u>is an honourable man;</u> **all that he saith cometh surely to pass** *(prophecy and word of wisdom)*: **now let us go thither; peradventure he can shew us our way that we should go...** 9 (Beforetime in Israel, when a man went to enquire of God, thus he spake, **Come, and let us go to the <u>seer</u>: for he that is now called a Prophet was beforetime called a <u>Seer</u>)**...

19 **And Samuel answered Saul, and said, I am the seer:** go up before me unto the high place; for ye shall eat with me today, and tomorrow I will let thee go, **and will tell thee all that is in thine heart. 20 And as for thine asses that were lost three days ago, set not thy mind on them; for they are found. <u>And on whom is all</u> <u>the desire of Israel?</u> Is it not on thee, and on all thy father's house?** *(Israel will love him as their*

King) 21 And Saul answered and said, Am not I a Benjamite, of the smallest of the tribes of Israel? and my family the least of all the families of the tribe of Benjamin? wherefore then speakest thou so to me?"

Before Saul left, the Prophet Samuel anointed him King over Israel —**1 Samuel 10:1:**

> **"Then Samuel took a vial of oil, and poured it upon his head, and kissed him, and said, Is it not because <u>the LORD hath anointed thee to be captain</u> *(King)* <u>over his inheritance?</u>"**

This was how Saul went from being a regular guy to become the first King of Israel —**the Word of a prophet <u>to a man</u> and <u>to a nation</u>.** If the children of Israel did not regard the Prophet Samuel as a prophet of God, they would not have received Saul as their King. People place their hopes in the Word of God that comes from God's true prophets; they hang on to every bit of the Word because according to the Lord, <u>it is life</u>. I have seen in my personal experience that the Word of God to me and through me is life and hope. For example:

> *I was in one of the African countries to minister and my flight arrived at about 5 pm and I checked into the hotel at about 7 pm with the instruction from my host to get some rest but at about 7:30 pm, there was a knock on my door. When I opened the door, it was the very person who told me to get some rest and she had a couple with her. **She apologized for disturbing my rest as she informed me that in her country, people get seriously excited when a prophet or a prophetess comes into the city.***

> *I was there to minister to the women in Parliament and she informed me that the word was out that a prophetess was in town. As she was speaking, the lady that came with*

*her began to cry and her husband started trying to comfort her. I asked was wrong and the husband informed me that their daughter went out the day before and had not been seen since. According to him, there was a serial killer loose in the city and the dead bodies of about six young girls had been discovered in the past several months. Naturally, they were afraid for their daughter's safety and he then informed me that their hope came alive when they heard that a prophetess was in the city and that **they have come to ask the Lord to tell them through me where their daughter was**!*

*On this day, I saw the importance of occupying the Office of the Prophet in the Kingdom of God. Before the man could finished posing the question, I heard the **Holy Spirit** declare very authoritatively, "**She is at her boyfriend's house and she will come home tomorrow at 5 pm!**" I said to the man and his wife, your daughter is at her boyfriend's house and she will be home tomorrow at 5 pm. The husband said to me, "**That is impossible because we looked at her boyfriend's house and she was not there and her boyfriend is part of the search party that is looking for her.**" I told him that the **Holy Spirit** cannot lie and I instructed them to go home and wait for her. True to God's Word, they were back at my hotel at about 8 pm the next day to inform me that their daughter came back home at 5 pm as the Lord said and that truly; she was hiding at her boyfriend's house. She told her parents that she knew her father will kill her for spending the night at her boyfriend's house so when they came looking for her there, she hid herself.*

The same night that my host brought the couple to hear the Word of the Lord concerning their daughter, she came again with another visitor. This time, one of the Members of Parliament wanted me to come and pray in the House of Parliament. I just assumed that she wanted me to pray for her in her office but when we got into her office, she *informed me that one of their Members of Parliament had dropped dead at 8 am that day and that she wanted to take me to the morgue **"to wake him up."** She made the request without any second thought that it was impossible or difficult for a Prophetess to raise the dead; so we headed to the morgue…*

The Fruit of the Spirit

God expects us to bring forth the fruit of the Holy Spirit in our daily lives and in order to accomplish this task, we need to know what the <u>fruit</u> of the Spirit is. We find the answer in **Galatians 5:22-23** because the different aspects of the "Fruit of the **Holy Spirit**" <u>are listed </u>for us there:

> "But **the fruit of the Spirit is love, joy, peace, longsuffering, gentleness, goodness, faith,** 23 **Meekness, temperance**: against such there is no law."

Below is a brief description of each fruit**.**
1. **Love** *(you are to love everyone; even your enemies)*
2. **Joy** *(He gives us reasons to be joyful; God comforts us even when we are mourning)*
3. **Peace** *(peace makers are called children of God)*
4. **Longsuffering** *(enduring to the end)*
5. **Gentleness** *(being willing to walk away when you are reviled; speaking godly words)*
6. **Goodness** *(doing good and not rewarding evil for evil)*
7. **Faith** *(Believing God's Word, you may be poor and destitute by society's standards but you can be rich in faith; faith helps you to become wealthy spiritually and physically)*
8. **Meekness** *(patience or submissive humbleness to the Word of God)*
9. **Temperance** *(thinking before you speak or act; hold your peace even when you are in a volatile situation)*

The Lord also stressed the need for us to have the fruit of the **Holy Spirit** in our daily lives as well **as demonstrate other godly attributes** that are also outlined in **Matthew 5:1-45:**

> "And seeing the multitudes, he went up into a mountain: and when he was set, his disciples came unto him: 2 And he opened his mouth, and taught them, saying, 3 Blessed are the **poor in spirit**: <u>for theirs is the kingdom of heaven</u> *(they have faith)*. 4 Blessed are **they that mourn**: <u>for they shall be comforted</u> *(joy)*. 5 Blessed are the **meek**: <u>for they shall inherit the earth</u>. 6 Blessed are they which do **hunger and thirst after righteousness**: <u>for they shall be filled</u>. 7 Blessed are the **merciful**: <u>for they shall obtain mercy</u>.
>
> 8 Blessed are the **pure in heart**: <u>for they shall see God</u>. 9 Blessed are the **peacemakers**: <u>for they shall be called the children of God</u>. 10 Blessed are they which are **persecuted for righteousness' sake: for theirs is the kingdom of heaven** *(you are to show gentleness)*. 11 Blessed are ye, when **men shall revile you, and persecute you, and shall say all manner of evil against you falsely, for my sake** *(you are to show temperance)*. 12 Rejoice, and be exceeding glad: <u>for great is your reward in heaven</u>: for so persecuted they the prophets which were before you *(you are to be longsuffering knowing what awaits you in heaven)*...
>
> 43 Ye have heard that it hath been said, Thou shalt love thy neighbour, and hate thine enemy. 44 **But I say unto you, <u>Love your enemies</u>,** <u>bless them that curse you, do good to them that hate you, and pray for them which despitefully use you, and persecute you;</u> 45 That ye may be the children of your Father

which is in heaven: for he maketh his sun to rise on the evil and on the good, and sendeth rain on the just and on the unjust."

According to the Lord, manifesting these godly attributes; especially when people rise up against us, actually earns us rewards from Him. For example, **being hungry and thirsty for righteousness** (having a desire to know and live by God's Word) opens the door for the Lord to fill us with knowledge while **showing mercy** (forgiving or letting people off the hook) earns us mercy when we need it ourselves. Those who walk with a **pure heart** (having a heart devoid of malice, envy, lusts, covetousness, and all the other works of the flesh) will enable them to always see God move on their behalf; at the end, they also behold His face! Again, only the **Holy Spirit** will help us do these things. There are other godly attributes in the scriptures and it is our responsibility to seek them out, to know them and to do them.

Chapter 8
The Holy Spirit is the Grace of God

The Lord Jesus told us in **John 15:5** <u>that without Him, we can do nothing</u>. Therefore, we need to learn about the **grace** of God that the **Holy Spirit** gives us:

> "I am the vine, ye are the branches: He that abideth in me, and I in him, the same bringeth forth much fruit: **for without me ye can do nothing.**"

The Lord gave us the **Holy Spirit** to help us on a daily basis as we are going to see in this chapter. We need Him every day of our lives and in every area of our lives.

He Make Us Bold and Fearless

<u>Grace is the divine ability that God gives us to be able to do the impossible or to accomplish tasks that defy the limitations of human abilities</u>. When the **Holy Spirit** comes into our lives, He becomes **the grace of God that enables us to do all that the Lord has commanded us to.** This is why the Lord told the disciples in **Luke 24:49** to stay in Jerusalem until they receive the <u>power from on high</u> that will enable them to successfully and courageously accomplish all the things that He commanded them:

> "And, behold, <u>I send the promise of my Father</u> (the Holy Spirit) <u>upon you</u>: **but tarry ye in the city of Jerusalem, until ye be endued with power from on high.**"

God uses the **Holy Spirit** to get things done and if you are going to be a witness of the Gospel today, you also need the help of the **Holy Spirit**. The Lord's promise that the disciples will be <u>endued with power from on high</u> was fulfilled in **Acts**

2:2-4; the day that the **Holy Spirit** came upon them and they were filled with the power of God — the **Holy Spirit:**

> "And when the <u>day of Pentecost</u> was fully come, they were all with one accord in one place. 2 <u>And suddenly there came a sound from heaven as of a rushing mighty wind, and it filled all the house where they were sitting. 3 And there appeared unto them cloven tongues like as of fire, and it sat upon each of them.</u> 4 **And <u>they were all filled with the Holy Ghost,</u> and began to speak with other tongues, as the Spirit gave them utterance…**"

The **Holy Spirit** simply filled them up with Himself and **He gave them boldness.** He also gave them His nine gifts that I discussed in the previous chapter and **He enabled Peter to minister without fear.** We can see the difference that He made in **Apostle Peter** in **Acts 2:12-24** after Peter received the **Holy Spirit** on the Day of Pentecost:

> "And they were all amazed, and were in doubt, saying one to another, What meaneth this? 13 Others mocking said, These men are full of new wine. 14 **But Peter, standing up with the eleven, <u>lifted up his voice, and said unto them,</u> Ye men of Judaea, and all ye that dwell at Jerusalem, be this known unto you, and hearken to my words: 15 For these are not drunken, as ye suppose, seeing it is but the third hour of the day.**
>
> 16 But this is that which was spoken by the prophet Joel; 17 And it shall come to pass in the last days, saith God, I will pour out of my Spirit upon all flesh: and your sons and your daughters shall prophesy, and your young men shall see

visions, and your old men shall dream dreams: 18 And on my servants and on my handmaidens I will pour out in those days of my Spirit; and they shall prophesy…

22 **Ye men of Israel, hear these words;** Jesus of Nazareth, a man approved of God among you by miracles and wonders and signs, which God did by him in the midst of you, as ye yourselves also know: 23 **Him, being delivered by the determinate counsel and foreknowledge of God, ye have taken, and by wicked hands have crucified and slain:** 24 **Whom God hath raised up, having loosed the pains of death: because it was not possible that he should be holden of it.**"

Before this day and at the trial of the Lord Jesus, <u>Peter denied knowing the Lord three times</u> because he was afraid but after being <u>endued with power from on High</u>, he was a changed man. Also, after healing the lame man at the "Gate Beautiful," Peter again by the power of the **Holy Spirit** looked at the Jews fearlessly as he spoke boldly to them; he let them know that they had crucified the <u>Holy One</u> in ignorance. Below is how it happened in **Acts 3:1-16:**

"Now Peter and John went up together into the temple at the hour of prayer, being the ninth hour. 2 And a certain man lame from his mother's womb was carried, whom they laid daily at the gate of the temple which is called Beautiful, to ask alms of them that entered into the temple; 3 Who seeing Peter and John about to go into the temple asked an alms. 4 <u>And Peter, fastening his eyes upon him with John, said, Look on us.</u>

5 And he gave heed unto them, expecting to receive something of them. 6 **Then Peter said,**

Silver and gold have I none; but such as I have give I thee: In the name of Jesus Christ of Nazareth rise up and walk. *7* And he took him by the right hand, and lifted him up: and immediately his feet and ankle bones received strength. *8* And he leaping up stood, and walked, and entered with them into the temple, walking, and leaping, and praising God. *9* And all the people saw him walking and praising God:

10 And they knew that it was he which sat for alms at the Beautiful gate of the temple: and they were filled with wonder and amazement at that which had happened unto him. *11* And as the lame man which was healed held Peter and John, all the people ran together unto them in the porch that is called Solomon's, greatly wondering. *12* And when Peter saw it, he answered unto the people, Ye men of Israel, why marvel ye at this? or why look ye so earnestly on us, as though by our own power or holiness we had made this man to walk?

13 The God of Abraham, and of Isaac, and of Jacob, the God of our fathers, hath glorified his Son Jesus; whom ye delivered up, and denied him in the presence of Pilate, when he was determined to let him go. *14* But ye denied the Holy One and the Just, and desired a murderer to be granted unto you; *15* And killed the Prince of life, whom God hath raised from the dead; whereof we are witnesses. *16* And his name through faith in his name hath made this man strong, whom ye see and know: yea, the faith which is by him hath given him this perfect soundness in the presence of you all."

This was the same Peter who about 40 days prior denied Jesus before a little maid and could not stand up for what He believed. From the boldness displayed by Peter, you can see why the Lord Jesus told the disciples to *"tarry in Jerusalem until they are endued with power from on high."* Under the power of the **Holy Spirit**, we can do things that used to make us fearful and we can go beyond our human knowledge and abilities to accomplish the impossible. He is our boldness; the grace from God.

The **Holy Spirit** gives us **courage** and **He helps us defy the obstacles that we see in the natural** so that we can charge forth to carry out the "great commission" (Mark 16:15-18) or what the Lord commanded us. We are not to be intimidated by people or their position and we are not to think of how we are going to answer the questions that they pose to us because the **Holy Spirit** is the one that will give us the answer as stated in **Mark 13:11:**

> "But when they shall lead you, and deliver you up, take no thought beforehand what ye shall speak, neither do ye premeditate: but whatsoever shall be given you in that hour, that speak ye: **for it is not ye that speak, but the Holy Ghost.**"

The Lord Jesus emphasized the need for <u>fearlessness</u> on our part because in Him, we receive the <u>peace that helps us overcome fear</u>. He told us that He has given us this peace in **John 14:27:**

> "Peace I leave with you, my peace I give unto you: not as the world giveth, give I unto you. Let not your heart be troubled, neither let it be afraid."

It also took the grace of God for Saul and Barnabas to carry out their several missionary journeys as recorded in **Acts 13:2-5:**

"As they ministered to the Lord, and fasted, **the Holy Ghost said, Separate me Barnabas and Saul for the work whereunto I have called them.** 3 And when they had fasted and prayed, and **laid their hands on them** *(impartation of the grace of God)*, they sent them away. 4 So they, being sent forth by the Holy Ghost, departed unto Seleucia; and from thence they sailed to Cyprus. 5 And when they were at Salamis, they preached the word of God in the synagogues of the Jews: and they had also John to their minister."

He Helped the Lord Jesus to Offer His Blood to God

As the **grace** from God, the **Holy Spirit** is the one that actually helped the **Lord Jesus** to make atonement for our sins. **God the Father** was in heaven when the Lord Jesus was in the grave but from heaven, He sent **His Spirit** on the third day into hell to raise Him up from the dead. In other words, **it took the Holy Spirit to raise the Lord Jesus up from the dead** and the Bible tells us in **Hebrews 9:13-15** that the **Lord Jesus through the Holy Spirit then took His blood and went and presented it to God the Father on our behalf as an atonement:**

"For if the blood of bulls and of goats, and the ashes of an heifer sprinkling the unclean, sanctifieth to the purifying of the flesh: 14 **How much more shall the blood of Christ, <u>who through the eternal Spirit</u> offered himself without spot to God, purge your conscience from dead works to serve the living God?**

15 And for this cause he is the mediator of the new testament, that by means of death, for the redemption of the transgressions that were under the first testament, they which are called might receive the promise of eternal inheritance."

In the physical, it may have seemed on the day of the Lord's crucifixion that all His blood was spilled and left on the ground but the truth is that not a drop of the Lord Jesus' blood was wasted. Yes, it dropped on the ground to cleanse even the earth but the **Holy Spirit** gathered every bit of it and the Lord Jesus took it before **God the Father** in the Holy of Holies to fulfill His righteous requirement in **Genesis 9:6** and **Ezekiel 18:4** that say respectively that, *"whoso sheddeth man's blood, by man shall his blood be shed: for in the image of God made he man"* and *"the soul that sinneth, it shall die."*

This is why it was necessary for the Lord Jesus to take His own blood and present it to His Father saying *(paraphrasing)*, *"My blood is sufficient for them; so let them go because I took responsibility for their sin against you."* This was how the Lord Jesus satisfied God's righteous requirement for us. Today, and still by the working of the **Holy Spirit**, when God sees us, **He sees us as being washed in the blood of His Son and declares us not guilty of our sin (rebellion) against Him.**

He Helped the Lord Jesus to Become Our High Priest

It was by the **grace** of God (Holy Spirit) that the Lord Jesus became our High Priest. The scriptures tell us in **Hebrews 5:5-10** that **God the Father** made the Lord Jesus a Priest forever after the order of Melchisedec (order of everlasting life):

> **"So also Christ glorified not himself to be made an high priest; but he that said unto him, Thou art my Son, today have I begotten thee. 6 As he saith also in another place, Thou art a priest for ever after the order of Melchisedec.** 7 Who in the days of his flesh, when he had offered up prayers and supplications with strong crying and tears unto him that was able to save him from death, and was heard in that he feared; 8 Though he were a Son, yet learned

he obedience by the things which he suffered; *9*
And being made perfect, he became the author
of eternal salvation unto all them that obey him;
10 **Called of God an high priest after the order
of Melchisedec."**

To understand what happened to the disciples on the **Day of
Pentecost**, you need to read **Hebrews 1:8-12** below because
it talks about **the day that the Lord Jesus was <u>formerly
anointed as our High Priest</u>** upon His return to heaven. God
the Father not only made Him **LORD** and **GOD**, He also
installed Him as our **High Priest** and it was **the anointing on
His head as our High Priest** (the Holy Spirit) that flowed on
to His body (His disciples or the Church) on earth on the Day
of Pentecost:

> "But unto the **Son** *(Jesus)* **he** *(God the Father)* **saith,
> Thy throne, <u>O God,</u> is forever and ever: a
> sceptre of righteousness is the sceptre of thy
> kingdom**. *9* Thou hast loved righteousness, and
> hated iniquity; <u>therefore **God, even thy God** *(God
> the Father)*, **hath anointed thee** *(Jesus)* **with the oil
> of gladness above thy fellows** *(humanity)*.</u>
>
> *10* And, **<u>Thou, Lord</u>** *(Jesus)*, <u>in the beginning hast
> laid the foundation of the earth; and the heavens
> are the works of thine hands</u>: *(the Word of God)*
> *11* they shall perish; but thou remainest *(eternal)*;
> and they all shall wax old as doth a garment; *12*
> And as a vesture shalt thou fold them up, and
> they shall be changed: **but thou art the same,
> and <u>thy years shall not fail</u>** *(33 1/2 years old forever;
> no more aging)*."

<u>**The Anointing of the Lord Jesus in heaven**</u> was like the
<u>Anointing of Aaron as High Priest by Moses</u> — the oil flowed
from His head down to His beard and then to His body as
recorded in Psalm 133. **The Lord Jesus needed to be installed
as our High Priest in heaven because offering blood to God**

the Father in the Holy of Holies is a function that <u>only</u> the High Priest is allowed to perform. No one else is allowed into the Holy of Holies to offer a blood sacrifice. I wrote about this in my book titled, *Experiencing the depths of Jesus Christ, chapter 15, page 146.* Below is an excerpt:

"<u>**By the single act of taking His own blood into heaven and into the Holy of Holies on our behalf, the Lord Jesus had become our High Priest.**</u> **Therefore, God the Father had to pour the anointing oil upon Him as it is required in the installation of a new High Priest.** <u>It was the overflow of the anointing on the Lord Jesus as our High Priest (head of the Church) that the believers received on earth on the **Day of Pentecost**</u>. We see this in **Psalm 133:2:**

> '**It is like the precious <u>ointment upon the head, that ran down upon the beard, even Aaron's beard</u>** *(the High Priest)*: **that went down to the skirts of his garments** *(his body i.e., the Church).*'

The Lord Jesus' role on our behalf as our **LORD, God**, and **High Priest** was formally activated or implemented in both heaven and earth on the **Day of Pentecost.**"

You should also read this book about *Experiencing the Depths of Jesus Christ* in detail if you have not already done so.

He is the Spirit of Wisdom and Counsel

The Bible talks about the <u>**seven spirits of the Lord**</u>. When you analyze them, you will see that they are actually the operations of the **Holy Spirit and they listed in Isaiah 11:2:**

> "And the **spirit of the LORD** *(the Holy Spirit)* **shall rest upon him**, the spirit of **wisdom** and **understanding**, the spirit of **counsel** and **might**, the spirit of **knowledge** and of the **fear of the LORD**…"

The scripture you just read reveals to us the different ways that the **Holy Spirit** helps us. He is the one that gives us <u>wisdom,</u> <u>understanding,</u> <u>counsel,</u> <u>might,</u> <u>knowledge</u> and <u>teaches us</u> to walk in the fear of the Lord. **What this means is that without the Holy Spirit, we cannot even walk in the fear of the Lord to obey His commandments or live by His Word.** As I stated before, the Bible tells us in **1 Corinthians 2:13-14** that the things of God are foolishness to those <u>who are not</u> in Christ and who rely on their intellects to understand them:

> "<u>Which things also we speak, not in the words</u> <u>which man's wisdom teacheth, but which the</u> <u>Holy Ghost teacheth; comparing spiritual things</u> <u>with spiritual.</u> *14* **But the natural man receiveth not the things of the Spirit of God: for they are foolishness unto him: neither can he know them, because they are spiritually discerned.**"

We see **Romans 8:6-8** stating the same thing in a different way:

> "**For to be carnally minded is death**; but to be spiritually minded is life and peace. *7* **Because the carnal mind is enmity against God: for it is not subject to the law of God, neither indeed can be.** *8* <u>So then they that are in the flesh cannot</u> <u>please God.</u>"

The **Holy Spirit** is truly God's grace upon our lives and we need Him in our daily lives. Simply put; without Him, we are sunk!

He is the Spirit of Liberty

By the power of the **Holy Spirit**, God uses the believers in His Son **Jesus Christ** to deliver those that are held in captivity by the devil; be it in their health, finances, relationships, general prosperity or business endeavors. As a result, we the believers are God's instrument to get people out of these various forms of captivity and also to help them find eternal life. This is why we are told in **1 Corinthians 3:17** that "**the Lord is that Spirit: and where the Spirit of the Lord is, there is liberty.**" We are also told in both **Isaiah 61:1** and in **Luke 4:18** that God has anointed the believers to go forth and to set the oppressed and the captives free:

> "**The Spirit of the Lord is upon me, because he hath anointed me** to preach the gospel to the poor; he hath sent me to heal the brokenhearted, **to preach deliverance to the captives,** and recovering of sight to the blind, **to set at liberty them that are bruised.**"

It does not matter what the devil and life has brought against a person; **God has anointed us** (given us the **Holy Spirit**) **to be able to heal, deliver, set them at liberty and release life and prosperity to them.** We are commanded in **Galatians 5:1** to stand in the liberty that we received from the Lord:

> "Stand fast therefore in the liberty wherewith Christ hath made us free, and be not entangled again with the yoke of bondage."

God Used the Holy Spirit to Create a New Body for Jesus

You have to remember that before the Lord Jesus died, **His face and body were badly marred beyond recognition** as stated in **Isaiah 52:14:**

> "As many were astonied at thee; **his visage was so marred more than any man, and his form more than the sons of men.**"

The Bible tells us in **Ephesians 1:19-21** that God had to make a new body for Him at His resurrection and as a result, He looked very different from the Jesus that they had seen working miracles and wonders on earth and on the Cross:

"And what is the exceeding greatness of his power to us-ward who believe, **according to the <u>working of his mighty power</u>, 20 <u>Which he wrought in Christ</u>, when he raised him from the dead** (*God created a new body for Christ*)**, and set him at his own right hand in the heavenly places,** 21 Far above all principality, and power, and might, and dominion, and every name that is named, not only in this world, but also in that which is to come."

God's "ultimate recreation of man" was done on the day that He fashioned a new body for Christ —this is the body that all believers will receive on the <u>day of rapture</u>! It is a body created by the **Holy Spirit** and not the body that God originally created from clay. As for us, we were originally created of clay in the 1ˢᵗ Adam but we have been recreated in the 2ⁿᵈ Adam which is Christ hence we are a **"new creature"** (2 Corinthians 5:17). We shall be given a "glorious body" at Christ's return. As you have seen, **all of these events took place by the working of the Holy Spirit.**

The **Holy Spirit** is very important in the kingdom of God and we need Him in all that we do as true believers on earth today. He also worked through the Lord Jesus while He was physically here on earth and He works through us today. **Even now, the Lord moves between heaven and earth by the working of the Holy Spirit.**

He Enabled the Lord Jesus to Enter Heaven Triumphantly

When the Holy Spirit raised the Lord from the dead, He enabled the Lord to take with Him to heaven all those who had died but who looked forward to His coming as the Messiah. These are the people who were <u>in Abraham's bosom</u> in the non-tormenting part of hell. Because Christ had not yet paid for "the sin of the world" with His blood, the devil held them in captivity (from Abel to the day that the Lord rose again from the dead) because of the Adamic authority that he had over them.

Adam willing gave the devil the authority to be Lord over the earth but when the Lord rose again in hell by the power of the Holy Spirit, He broke the bars of their captivity and set them free. This is why the Bible says that the Lord Jesus took captivity captive" in **Psalm 68:18** and in **Ephesians 4:8-10**. He did this by the power of the **Holy Spirit:**

> **"Wherefore he saith, When he ascended up on high, he led <u>captivity captive</u>, and gave gifts unto men.** *9* (Now that he ascended, what is it but that **he also <u>descended first into the lower parts of the earth</u>?** *10* **He that descended is the same also that ascended up far above all heavens, that he might fill all things."**

The Lord reentered heaven as a triumphant conqueror and He ascended into heaven with all the hosts of people that He had set free from death and the grave following behind Him! He reentered heaven as the **Lord of Hosts** because the whole hosts of them followed Him into heaven. We see His triumphant reentry into heaven recorded in **Psalms 24:7-10:**

> "Lift up your heads, O ye gates; and be ye lift up, ye everlasting doors; and the **King of glory** shall come in. *8* Who is this **King of glory? The LORD strong and mighty, the LORD mighty in battle.** *9* Lift up your heads, O ye gates; even lift them up, ye everlasting doors; and **the King of glory** shall come in. *10* Who is this **King of glory? The LORD of hosts** *(the hosts are the people that followed Him into heaven),* **he is the King of glory.** Selah."

The first time He went back into heaven, it was as God's lamb and He went into the Holy of Holies <u>to present His</u>

own blood as atonement to **God the Father** on our behalf. **At His second reentry on the day of His ascension, He went in as the "Conquering Warrior."** Hence the scripture above tells us that **the gatekeeper in heaven did not recognize the transformation that had taken place in Him (going from a Lamb to a Lion by the power of the Holy Spirit) and with a different boldness and an authoritative command**. No one had ever spoken this way before when entering heaven so the gatekeeper asked, **"Who is this king of glory"** and the Lord replied, **The LORD that is coming with a massive hosts of people, He is the King of glory!**

He Enabled Moses to Lead the Children of Israel

Moses was not really trained as a leader in Jewish customs, ministry, ways and commandments of God. He was just a prince in Egypt and he had been schooled in the ways of the Egyptians but he encountered God in Mount Sinai and God told him to go to Egypt and set His people (the children of Israel) free. In obedience to God, he went to Egypt and did a lot of "on the job training" as God used him to do miracles, signs, and wonders because he had faith. As you read about what he did in Egypt, you will see that God told him what to do and he went out and did it; because of his faith and obedience, the **Holy Spirit** manifested the outcome. The **Holy Spirit** was the one doing the miracles, signs and wonders through him and Aaron.

As he was in the wilderness bringing the children of Israel into "the land filled with milk and honey," he encountered various types of problems from the children of Israel because a lot of them had no faith and were very ungrateful. Every time things did not go the way they wanted, they cried, murmured and complained. As part of their murmuring, they would tell Moses how they had it so good in Egypt and how terrible it was for Moses to make them leave behind all their delicious cucumbers, meats and leeks. In other words, whenever things got tough, they would cry about all the good things that they had in Egypt and they would forget that they were slaves in Egypt.

Their crying, murmuring and complaining finally got to the point that Moses asked God to kill him rather than have him continue to lead them. **What Moses did not realize at this time was the tremendous Anointing (the Spirit of God) that was upon Him.** Therefore, God in His mercy <u>took of the Spirit that was upon Moses</u> and gave it to 70 other people! **In other words, Moses had more than enough grace and capacity (Anointing) for more than 70 people.** It is all recorded in **Numbers 11:10-15, 25:**

> "Then Moses heard the people weep throughout their families, every man in the door of his tent: and the anger of the LORD was kindled greatly; Moses also was displeased. *11* And Moses said unto the LORD, **Wherefore hast thou afflicted thy servant? and wherefore have I not found favour in thy sight, that thou layest the burden of all this people upon me?**
>
> *12* **Have I conceived all this people? have I begotten them, that thou shouldest say unto me, Carry them in thy bosom, as a nursing father beareth the sucking child, unto the land which thou swarest unto their fathers?** *13* **Whence should I have flesh to give unto all this people? for they weep unto me, saying, Give us flesh, that we may eat.**
>
> *14* <u>**I am not able to bear all this people alone, because it is too heavy for me.**</u> *15* <u>**And if thou deal thus with me, kill me, I pray thee, out of hand, if I have found favour in thy sight; and let me not see my wretchedness**</u>...
>
> *25* And the LORD came down in a cloud, and spake unto him *(Moses)*, **and took of the spirit**

> **that was upon him, and gave it unto the seventy elders:** and <u>it came to pass, that, when the spirit rested upon them, they prophesied, and did not cease.</u>"

The seventy elders became the people that helped Moses to carry out judgment on minor cases so that Moses did not have to wear himself out by hearing cases from morning to night every day. Before this time, even Moses' father-in-law told him that the work he was doing was too much for one man because he saw that Moses was judging the people from morning to night every day. As we read in Exodus 18:13-24, he advised Moses to set up <u>magistrate judges</u> to help him out.

Both Moses and the people that God raised up to help him out on a daily basis were able to perform their function solely by the Anointing of the **Holy Spirit**. What we have today in our court systems; where minor civil and minor criminal matters are heard at the magistrate level and the more serious cases by the higher courts up to the courts of appeals, is the direct result of this Judeo court system began by Moses.

Waiting on the Holy Spirit before Starting a Ministry

Let the **Holy Spirit** process and anoint you for ministry work; do not go ahead of Him or lag behind Him. **When God calls you to any ministry work, He makes you wait until He has processed and anointed you.** This is why I tell people not to hastily pursue a ministry but to make sure that God has processed and anointed them first. We all need to allow the **Holy Spirit** to give us what we need to accomplish what we are asking God to do with us in terms of ministry work. We must all trust Him because He knows when to release us into ministry. It takes the **Holy Spirit** to do all the things that we need done concerning your ministry. Therefore, we should all make the **Holy Spirit** our best friend.

Chapter 9
The Holy Spirit is the Spirit of Mercy and Judgment

The Holy Spirit as the Spirit of Mercy

The **Holy Spirit** is the agent of God's MERCY. When **God the Father** wants to bring forth an act of <u>mercy</u>, He sends His **Holy Spirit** as we see concerning His plan of salvation for us. When it came time for God to implement His salvation plan for humanity, He sent His **Word** into the womb of a 16 year old virgin named Mary — **Luke 1:35**. Then, the **Holy Spirit** incubated the **Word** in Mary's womb and 9 months later, the **Word** came out as a baby named **Jesus**:

> "And the angel answered and said unto her, **The <u>Holy Ghost</u>** shall come upon thee, and the **power of the Highest** shall overshadow thee: **therefore also that holy thing which shall be born of thee shall be called the Son of God.**"

Also, in **Matthew 1:20-23**, we learned that **God** spoke to Joseph (Mary's espoused husband) in a dream when Joseph was contemplating divorcing Mary as a result of her out-of-wedlock pregnancy. He told Joseph that the child in Mary's womb was **"of the Holy Spirit."** Below is the scriptural record of how **God** spoke to Joseph:

> "But while he *(Joseph)* thought on these things *(secretly divorcing Mary)*, behold, the angel of the Lord appeared unto him in a dream, saying, Joseph, thou son of David, fear not to take unto thee Mary thy wife: **for that which is conceived in her is of the Holy Ghost.** *21* <u>And she shall bring forth a son, and thou shalt call his name JESUS</u>: **for he shall save his people from their sins.**

22 Now all this was done, that it might be fulfilled which was spoken of the Lord by the prophet, saying, 23 **Behold, a virgin shall be with child, and shall bring forth a son, and they shall call his name Emmanuel, which being interpreted is, God with us."**

God's greatest MERCY to humanity is <u>the sacrifice of His only begotten Son on the Cross for the SIN of the world.</u> The truth of the matter is that God actually displayed His MERCY for us in Adam and Eve (for we are their descendants) on the day that they sinned in the Garden of Eden. **You will notice when you read the scripture about their sin that God gave both Adam and Eve the opportunity to repent for what they had done but <u>they did not repent.</u>** Instead, they went into the blame game; Adam blamed Eve and Eve blamed the serpent (the devil). God therefore had a choice to make: destroy them or have mercy on them.

Despite their blame game, **God in His LOVE and MERCY for them and their descendants (us); took a LAMB (Jesus) and slew Him in the Garden of Eden and He used both the blood and the skin of the LAMB to clothe Adam and Eve — Genesis 3:8-21:**

"And they heard the voice of the LORD God walking in the garden in the cool of the day: and Adam and his wife hid themselves from the presence of the LORD God amongst the trees of the garden. 9 And the LORD God called unto Adam, and said unto him, Where art thou? 10 And he said, I heard thy voice in the garden, and I was afraid, because I was naked; and I hid myself *(their sin made them feel naked and ashamed).* 11 And he said, **Who told thee that thou wast naked? Hast thou eaten of the tree, <u>whereof I commanded thee that thou shouldest not eat?</u>**

12 <u>And the man said,</u> **The woman whom thou gavest to be with me, she gave me of the tree, and I did eat.** 13 <u>And the LORD God said unto the woman,</u> **What is this that thou hast done?** <u>And the woman said,</u> **The serpent beguiled me, and I did eat**... 20 <u>And Adam called his wife's name Eve; because she was the mother of all living.</u> 21 **Unto Adam also and to his wife did the LORD God make** <u>coats of skins</u> *(from the Lamb)*, **and clothed them.**"

It was right there and then in the Garden of Eden that God's MERCY was extended to all humanity! We all sinned in Adam and we all deserved death but God chose to extend His mercy to us by saving us. Therefore, we can safely proclaim what the Bible says about the Lord Jesus in **Revelation 13:8** that He is *"the Lamb slain from the foundation of the world."* Although God accomplished this work of redemption for us right after Adam and Eve sinned (within the 6 days of His "work of creation" and rested on the 7th day as recorded in the book of Genesis), <u>it took thousands of years for God's perfect time</u> of manifesting the work in the physical realm to arrive.

When the time finally arrived, it also took the working of the **Holy Spirit** to accomplish it all in the earth realm using the child (Jesus) of a 16 year old girl! **Just think about it, God Almighty making Himself a baby in the womb of an earthly woman in order to make Himself a human being so that He can save humanity from the bondage to sin and death.** It is quite an accomplishment by the **One and Only <u>Almighty God</u>. He could have destroyed Adam and Eve (and us in them) as He did the Pre-Adamic beings that occupied the earth in the days of Lucifer** *(see my book titled, How to Discern and Expel Evil Spirits for details about this topic).* We therefore, must all **appreciate** the scripture in **Romans 5:8-12** which says:

"**But God commendeth his love toward us** *(showed us His love)*, **in that, <u>while we were yet sinners</u>** *(Adam and Eve did not repent of their sin),* **Christ died for us.** 9 <u>Much more then, being now justified **by his blood**, we shall be saved from wrath through him.</u> 10 **For if, when we were enemies, we were reconciled to God by the death of his Son, much more, being reconciled, we shall be saved by his life.** 11 And not only so, but we also joy in God through our Lord Jesus Christ, by whom we have now received the atonement. 12 **Wherefore, as by one man sin entered into the world, and death by sin; and so death passed upon all men, for that all have sinned.**"

Just as Adam and Eve were clothed with the skin of God's Lamb in the Garden of Eden, today, we who believe in God's Lamb (Jesus), are also clothed with His blood and His skin — we have put on Christ:

"**For as many of you as have been baptized into Christ have put on Christ**" (Galatians 3:27).

The Holy Spirit as the Spirit of Judgment

The Lord Jesus told us that He Himself does nothing except what He sees His Father do. He also told us that **the Father** has committed all judgment to Him. The **Holy Spirit** was the one that helped the Lord to pronounce righteous judgments while He was on earth as He himself declared in **John 5:19-22**:

"**Then answered Jesus and said unto them, Verily, verily, I say unto you, The Son can do nothing of himself, but what he seeth the Father do**: for what things soever he doeth, these also doeth the Son likewise 20 For the Father loveth the Son, and <u>sheweth him all things that himself doeth</u> *(by the Holy Spirit)…* 22 **For the Father judgeth no man, but hath committed all judgment unto the Son."**

The **way it worked was that the Holy Spirit** would show the Lord Jesus what **God the Father** was doing in heaven and the Lord Jesus will then do the same on earth. He also showed the Lord the Father's judgments concerning earthly matters. **In other words, the Holy Spirit helped the Lord to understand the Father's heart in all things including judgments.** The Lord then informed us that as the Father sent Him, so He also has sent us in **John 20:21:**

> "Then said Jesus to them again, Peace be unto you: **as my Father hath sent me, even so send I you.**"

In other words, right here on earth, **we are co-reigning with Christ by the power of the Holy Spirit** as stated in Romans 5:17 and Revelation 5:10. As a result, **we can proclaim** God's MERCY and God's JUDGMENT as stated in **1 Corinthians 2:15** — *"But he that is spiritual judgeth all things, yet he himself is judged of no man"* and also in **John 20:23:**

> **"Whosesoever sins ye remit, they are remitted unto them** *(Mercy)*; and **whosesoever sins ye retain, they are retained** *(Judgment).*"

Today, we are <u>**God's instruments of mercy and also His instruments of judgment**</u> of "all things ungodly" and we cannot shy away from the responsibility. The good news is that it is the Lord **Holy Spirit** that gives us the wisdom to carry out this task. It is not something that we can do by ourselves; remember what the Lord Jesus said, **"Without me ye can do nothing"** in John 15:5. We need both the wisdom and the help of the **Lord Holy Spirit**.

Chapter 10
The Holy Spirit is Our Another Comforter

The Lord Jesus is Our Comforter

Today, if there is anything that the world is in need of, it is comfort from God as people strive daily with sicknesses, diseases, poverty, lack, broken relationships or family and other afflictions from the devil. The Lord Jesus informed us in **Matthew 11:28-30** that He is **our first comforter** and He invited us to bring all our burdens and cares to Him as we can see below:

> **"Come unto me, all ye that labour and <u>are heavy laden</u>, and <u>I will</u> give you rest.** *29* <u>Take my yoke upon you</u>, and **learn of me**; for I am meek and lowly in heart: and **ye shall find <u>rest</u> unto your souls.** *30* **For my yoke is easy, and my burden is light."**

The Holy Spirit as the Another Comforter

Before His departure to heaven, the Lord Jesus promised in **John 14:16-26** to send us **another Comforter** —the **Holy Spirit** and He did so on the Day of Pentecost. Therefore, <u>the Holy Spirit</u> has been on earth to keep us, to teach us, to help us minster the Gospel, **to comfort** us and to guide us in all things until the Lord returns:

> **"And I will pray the Father, and he shall give you <u>another Comforter</u>, that he may abide with you forever;** *17* **Even the Spirit of truth;** whom the world cannot receive, because it seeth him not, neither knoweth him: but **ye know him; for <u>he dwelleth with you</u>, and <u>shall be in you</u>.** *18* **I will not leave you comfortless:** I will come to you... *26* **But <u>the Comforter</u>, <u>which is the Holy Ghost</u>,** whom the Father will send in my

name, **he shall teach you all things, and bring
all things to your remembrance, whatsoever I
have said unto you."**

Today, the Lord Jesus comes to us by the **Holy Spirit**. He
sends His comfort to us through the "Another Comforter"
— the **Holy Spirit**. Even when the Lord visits us personally
or in visions and dreams, it is still by the working of the
Holy Spirit.

The Holy Spirit as the Heavenly
Dove with Comforting Wings

Because He loves us, the Lord Jesus brings us **His
healing and comfort** by the working of the **Holy Spirit**
whenever we need it. I have met many people that have
seen the **Holy Spirit** come to them as our **Comforter** in the
form of a Dove. **The reason God sends Him as a Dove is
because the dove is a very gentle and tender bird. It loves
completely and it can be easily wounded. It cries when it
is wounded and is very patient.**

As our **Another Comforte**r, it is the **Holy Spirit** that
administers God's relief, healing and comfort to us when we
are in pain, in a difficult situation, or in need of healing. He
comes as **God's Heavenly Dove** with healing in His wings as
it is written in **Malachi 4:2:**

> "But unto you that fear my name shall the **Sun
> of righteousness** *(Jesus)* **arise with healing in
> his wings**; and ye shall go forth, and grow up
> as calves of the stall."

Do you remember that the **Holy Spirit** is also referred to as
the **Spirit of Christ?** Therefore, when the Lord Jesus comes
to us in times of sorrow, He comes by the **Holy Spirit**. For
example, when we have just lost a loved one, the Lord fulfills
His promise to us in **Matthew 5:5** through the **Holy Spirit:**

"Blessed are they that mourn: for they shall
be comforted."

As a result of the things that the **Holy Spirit** does for us, we
can safely say that He is the **Spirit of Comfort**. He gives us
God's Words to comfort us and others. We have just seen that
He also comes to comfort us when we are sorrowful, sick or
feeling alone.

My Experience of the Holy
Spirit as Our Comforter

*I thank God that I rarely get sick but I remember some
years ago when I was in bed with a cold and I was alone
and feeling sorry for myself. As I laid there in self-
pity, I must have dozed off but the gentle breeze of the
Holy Spirit woke me up and I opened my eyes in time
to see that the **Holy Spirit** as the **heavenly Dove** was
hovering with His wings spread over me. I was amazed
at the love that God has for me as the **Holy Spirit** was
flapping His wings ever so gently while releasing His
healing and comfort to me.*

*He healed me completely and I was up and about right after
He left. I was very touched to know that God cares when
I am not well and when I am feeling alone; and that He
loves me so much that He would send His **Holy Spirit** to
comfort me. My experience was a fulfillment of the Lord's
promise to us in the scripture in the book of Malachi above
— the Sun of righteousness arising over us with healing in
His wings!*

All Believers Can Feel the Comfort of the Holy Spirit

Every believer has the capacity to feel the comfort of the
Holy Spirit because He is with us in two ways; He **dwells
in us** and is **with us**. This implies both internal and external
habitation of the **Holy Spirit** in our lives. **The problem on**

our part is that God does not communicate with the human mind but with the human spirit. What this requires therefore, is a development of our **internal** (inner witness) and **external** (other believers) discernment skills but most believers do not challenge themselves to do this. As long as they attempt to communicate with God with their intellect, they will remain outside of His communication realm.

This is why it is difficult for those who are not yet born again to engage in communication with Him or to understand the ways that He communicates because **they usually expect the things of God to makes sense to them** <u>before</u> they can believe or act upon them. What they do not know is that God's communication level is higher than ours and as a result, He does not appeal to our human reasoning or intellect. **He is a Spirit and as such, He wants to talk to our human spirits and not our minds or our reasoning.** We have to learn to recognize when God is speaking to us through our inner witness and when He is using other believers to speak to us.

Chapter 11
The Holy Spirit is the Tender Side of God

He Relates to Us Like a Nursing Mother

The **Holy Spirit** is the tender side of **God** that functions like a mother because He is the nurturing, the caring, the soft and the gentle side of **God the Father** and the **Lord Jesus Christ**. In other words, the **Holy Spirit** manifests the gentler and tender side of **God** for us so that we can know that God is not only a Father to us but that He also has the qualities of a mother. Like a mother, He is able to nurture us and keep us. We see His declaration in **Isaiah 66:13** that He will manifest His tender and softer side to us in order to comfort us:

> "As one **whom his mother comforteth, so will I comfort you**; and ye shall be comforted in Jerusalem."

What God is saying here is that, mothers are known as the ones who comfort their children and one of the ways that a mother comforts her crying baby is to let the baby nurse on her breasts. Also, as part of her care-giving duties, she carries the baby, walks the baby and sings to the baby. Therefore, when it comes to being our care-giver, God treats us as a mother will treat her nursing child!

It is the **Holy Spirit** that **God** uses to manifest this caring and nurturing side of Himself. This is why He can promise us who believe in Him that as one whom his mother comforts, so will He comfort us. Also, the Prophet Isaiah said the following to us in **Isaiah 40:11**:

> "He shall feed his flock like a shepherd: he shall gather the lambs with his arm, and **carry them in his bosom**, and shall gently lead those that are with young."

As part of her care-giving duties, it is the mother that usually carries the little ones that are not yet able to walk long distances by themselves. In order words, when you take little children that are 1 or 2 years old outside, they will walk a little while and then, they want you to carry them. Without hesitation, the mother will just pick them up and carry them the rest of the way. **Therefore, what God is saying here is that like a mother, He will carry you all the way.** Like a mother, He will even be mindful of the women who are pregnant and will gently lead them as He carries the entire nation of Israel and now, the believers as well; He will not allow us to be "rocked" by turbulence or adverse conditions.

If you have ever visited or are living in a developing country, you will probably be able to relate to the hardships that pregnant women face on a daily basis as they endure the most hazardous car or bus rides on very bad and rocky roads. It is one of the most painful sights to me when I visit Nigeria. It is nerve racking to see a woman who is fully with child travel on these bad road conditions and I never cease to wonder if they will make it home safely. As a result of what I have seen, I think that it is very thoughtful of God to take note of how a pregnant or a nursing mother needs to be treated delicately. We see another really nice example of God's nurturing side in **Isaiah 49:15-16:**

> **"Can a woman forget her sucking child, that she should not have compassion on the son of her womb?** <u>yea, they may forget,</u> **yet will I not forget thee.** 16 Behold, **I have graven thee upon the palms of my hands;** <u>thy walls are continually before me.</u>"

In the scripture above, God is promising to care for us and to protect us better than a negligent mother cares for her children hence He says to us that even if our mothers forsake us, He will not forsake us. Most women will give their lives for their young children but some women have been known to abandon or forsake their young children. Some women have aborted or abandoned their children in garbage bags, trash cans, toilets, or some other awful places.

There are those who gave up their children for adoption; not to mention the ones that just simply walked away from their husbands and children.

There are mothers who have abandoned their children with their own mothers or their grandmothers and walked away without looking back. **God is saying here that even if your mother does any of the above things to you, He will be there for you.** In other words, He will not abandon us; even when our fathers and our mothers abandon us, He will be there for us! **Some men are equally guilty of these crimes as you will see in the scripture below but God is mostly addressing the nurturing roles of women as mothers here.** Even the aborted babies are taken by the Lord according to **Psalms 27:10:**

> "When my father and my mother forsake me,
> **then the LORD will take me up."**

He takes up all the aborted babies! This should be a great comfort to women who have aborted their babies and now regret doing so but it does not mean that you (men and women) should choose to abort your baby because God takes up aborted babies. It will be a willful sin if you do that.

Caution: I also want to issue a word of warning here concerning the nurturing side of **God the Father**. Referring to His nurturing side does not mean that God is woman or that you should refer to Him as she or her. In Christendom, we do not believe in the new age doctrine of mother god, mother earth, Gaia, etc. God manifests Himself as a man –the "Man of War" and not as woman. What this discussion in this chapter is showing us is that although God is a Father (a man); He has the ability to also nurture like a mother.

He is Like the 'Mother Hen'

The Lord Jesus came to physically manifest God's love to us and He was able to do this by the workings of the **Holy**

Spirit. He likened Himself to a **'mother hen'** in His attempt to show how He loved the children of Israel. The **Holy Spirit** helped Him to demonstrate and to cry out His love as we see in **Luke 13:34-36:**

> "O Jerusalem, Jerusalem, which killest the prophets, and stonest them that are sent unto thee; **how often would I have gathered thy children together, as a hen doth gather her brood under her wings, and ye would not!** 35 Behold, your house is left unto you desolate: and verily I say unto you, Ye shall not see me, until the time come when ye shall say, Blessed is he that cometh in the name of the Lord."

Not only does God nurture and care for us human beings as a mother does, He also cares about the animals and the birds. Look at how He revealed this side of Himself to us in **Job 38:39-41:**

> "**Wilt thou hunt the prey for the lion? or fill the appetite of the young lions,** 40 When they couch in their dens, and abide in the covert to lie in wait? 41 Who provideth for the raven his food? **when his young ones cry unto God, they wander for lack of meat.**"

By His Spirit, God is able to feed the animals in the wild! He manifests His love to His creation by the workings of the **Holy Spirit**.

My Experience of God's Loving Care for Animals

I know that God made all the animals but it never occurred to me that He paid attention to their particular needs until one evening at my mother's house:

On this occasion, I was home on a visit towards the end of the year and my mother had bought a big roaster that she intended to kill for a Christmas or New Year dinner for her pastor. It was several days before the dinner, so she tied the roaster to a pole on the side of the house.

I was sitting outside one evening and I began to watch the roaster and I noticed that Mom had ground up some corn and placed it before the roaster but it did not eat any of it. From the look of it, it seemed as though all the food that Mom tried to feed the roaster were barely eaten by the roaster for several days. In a way, I felt sorry for the roaster because it was only a few days away from being killed and I wondered if the roaster knew somehow. As dusk began to set in, I saw a <u>mother hen</u> with several of her young ones. They went by me and headed for the food that was in front of the roaster and when I saw them, I drove them away because they were trespassing.

*They ran away when I drove them away but not long after, they came back. I got up to drive them away again and the Lord said to me very gently, let them alone because "it is getting late and her young ones are hungry." **He told me not to drive them away and to let them eat so that they can go to bed!** I was shocked at the love that God has even for animals. It took the **Holy Spirit** to help me hear, understand and obey God's communication; most importantly, **to help me understand the depths of God's love for man and the rest of His creation.***

He is the Protective Hedge over Us

God built **a wall** or **a hedge of protection** (the Holy Spirit) around us to make sure that we are safe and secure from the devil and his wiles. This is why the devil cannot operate in our lives unless we give him permission to do so by breaking the hedge of protection that God placed around us. To illustrate this point, you need to read about the man named Job. He was a righteous man and he knew it but at the same time, God saw pride in Job and He knew that He needed to humble Job before He can elevate him any further.

As recorded in **Job 1:8-11**, the devil had previously gone on his own to launch an attack against Job but he saw that there was no way for him to get to Job to harm him because God had built a hedge of protection round about Job. Job was righteous but he was <u>full of himself</u>. If you do not believe this, just read about Job and you will see how he viewed himself and those around him. How do you deal with a man that is righteous but has a touch of pride? God always has a way to accomplish His work in us through the **Holy Spirit**. Therefore to humble Job, He just simply invited the devil against him but the **Holy Spirit** was still his hedge of protection:

> "And the LORD said unto Satan, <u>Hast thou</u> <u>considered my servant Job, that there is none</u> <u>like him in the earth, a perfect and an upright</u> <u>man, one that feareth God, and escheweth</u> <u>evil?</u> *9* **Then Satan answered the LORD, and** **said, Doth Job fear God for nought?** *10* **<u>Hast</u>** **<u>not thou made an hedge about him, and about</u>** **<u>his house, and about all that he hath on every</u>** **<u>side?</u> thou hast blessed the work of his hands,** **and his substance is increased in the land.** *11* But put forth thine hand now, and touch all that he hath, and he will curse thee to thy face."

God hates pride and He will invite the devil against anyone who walks in it. The quickest way to break God's hedge around us is to **commit an act of iniquity or sin**. Another way is to practice wickedness, witchcraft, divination, sorcery, join the occult or have family members who are in the occult such as Free Masonry, Bohemian Grove, Illuminati Groups, Eastern Star, Rosicrucian Order, Knights Templar, Satanic Covens, KKK, etc. The activities of these types of groups will break God's hedge about a person and their family and give the devil access into the person's life.

Chapter 12
The Holy Spirit is the Warrior Side of God

As I said earlier, **God the Father** is in heaven and His Son; the **Lord Jesus** has gone back to join Him but **God the Father** sends His Spirit — the **Holy Spirit** to accomplish whatever He wants done on earth. As a matter of fact, **God the Father** does nothing on earth except by **His Word**; the **Lord Jesus** and through the **Holy Spirit** because the **Holy Spirit** produces what **God's Word** says. **God the Father has given all creation (including the earth and every living thing in it) as a giant gift to His beloved Son.** To administer His vast dominion, the **Holy Spirit** enables the **Lord Jesus** to move or transact His Father's business in heaven and on earth. Through the **Holy Spirit**, the Lord can arise as the **Righteous Warrior** when He needs to.

He Helped Jesus Appear as "Captain of the Host of the Lord"

God promised to bring the children of Israel into a land that is "flowing with milk and honey" but when they got to Gilgal, they first had to be circumcised; become sanctified or separated to God. The circumcision was in reality, the activation of the covenant that the children of Israel have with God as the **Seed of Abraham**. As soon as they took on the sign of the covenant in their bodies (the circumcision), the Lord Jesus through the working of the **Holy Spirit** appeared to Joshua in the plain of Jericho. This was many years before His manifestation on earth as the Son of God.

Although God had promised to give the children of Israel the land, He also wanted them to learn warfare. What this meant was that they had to actively drive away all the "ites" and the "ikes" that were in the land of Canaan; **they had to go to war in order to posses what God had already given them by His promise.** It was while they were in the battlefield that Joshua saw a man with a sword that intrigued

<u>him</u>. Joshua went over to the man and he asked the man if He was their ally or an ally of their enemies — **Joshua 5:13-15:**

> "And it came to pass, when Joshua was by Jericho, **that he lifted up his eyes and looked, and, behold, there stood a man over against him with his sword drawn in his hand:** and Joshua went unto him, and said unto him, **Art thou for us, or for our adversaries?** 14 And <u>he said,</u> **Nay; but as <u>captain of the host of the LORD</u> am I now come. And Joshua fell on his face to the earth, and did worship, and said unto him, What saith my lord unto his servant?** 15 <u>And the captain of the LORD'S host said unto Joshua,</u> Loose thy shoe from off thy foot; for the place whereon thou standest is holy. And Joshua did so."

We can see from the Lord's response that He is <u>the Lord</u> and that <u>He is no respecter of persons</u>; He said "Nay;" meaning **No** to the question of whether He was for them or for their enemies. In other words, He said to Joshua, I have come as "Captain of the host of the Lord;" the children of Israel are the ones that have made a decision through their circumcision to be for Him. As a result, <u>the army of Israel</u> is therefore regarded as **the army of the Lord but the Lord is the Lord of all**. Because they have separated themselves to Him, He came by the power of the **Holy Spirit** as their Captain to lead them in battle but it does not mean that He hates the other human beings that are not Jews.

Upon realizing who was standing in front of him, Joshua fell on his face and worshipped Him and the Lord received the worship. The last time we saw the Lord Jesus doing this was when Moses was before Him in the burning bush in **Exodus 3:5-6**. The Lord Jesus appeared to Moses at the **Angel of the Lord** in the burning bush. For a detailed discussion of this topic, see the second book in this series of 3 books titled, *Experiencing the Depths of Jesus Christ, pages 38-42.*

Needless to say that we all have to be careful about who we give our worship to because in this particular instance, <u>this man</u> did not rebuke Joshua for worshipping him but instead, confirmed who Joshua believed him to be — the Lord! One thing that we always have to remember is that only God can receive worship and that any angel who receives worship will be banished instantly by God forever. Receiving the worship that was meant only for God was Lucifer's sin — he wanted to be like the **Most High** who sits on the sides of the north and receive worship! Also, he corrupted the Pre-Adamic beings that he was given charge over on earth by soliciting them to worship him instead of God. You can also read about these events in my book titled, ***How to Discern and Expel Evil Spirits***, *Chapter 2, pages 57-68.*

In short, we can say that Joshua had an encounter with the **Lord Jesus** in Jericho by the <u>power of the</u> **Holy Spirit**. He is the Spirit that God uses to wage war.

He Helped Jesus Show Up as the "Man of War"

In **Exodus 15:3**, we see God referred to by the title, **"Man of War."** As the **"Man of War,"** the Lord Jesus by the power of the **Holy Spirit** appeared physically and wrestled with Jacob all night. According to Him; even today, when someone proves to be very stubborn, He will **wrestle with that person** and He always wins because He is the **"Man of War:"**

> "**The LORD is a <u>man of war</u>**: the LORD is his name."

His goal is to save us from self-destruction, iniquities and sins. I remember Him telling me one day that He allowed me to go through a very hard time when I first began my <u>initial ministry</u> and I lost everything. I had to leave ministry to go get a job but I was angry with Him because I thought that I was doing good for Him and He let me down. It was about three years later that He came to help me understand what happened to me during those very hard times. He said to me, *"I; myself, I'm the one who wrestled with you concerning 'your ministry' because that was not the way that I had called you!"* **I was shocked because all the things that I thought were the works of the devil was actually God wrestling or at war with me to keep me from going the wrong way.** According to Him, He was pleased when I had to shut down that ministry but now I can understand why because the ministry that He gave me is totally different from the one that I had started by myself many years before.

He can go to war against a person, a city or a nation. As a matter of fact, He can go to war with the entire world if need be and a day is coming when the whole world will give an account to Him about all that they did while living on His earth rent free. God promised not to strive with man by His Spirit any longer. He made this promise after He destroyed the world that existed in Noah's days. He saved only Noah and his family and commanded them to repopulate the earth and to replenish it. After Noah offered Him a burnt sacrifice, God made the following promise to man and to every living thing on earth as recorded in **Genesis 6:3:**

> "And the LORD said, **My spirit shall not always strive with man**, for that he also is flesh: yet his days shall be an hundred and twenty years."

Through the Lord Jesus, God has extended <u>His grace and mercy</u> to humanity but He will war on our behalf against evil forces and He will wrestle with us when He sees us going the wrong way and we do not yield to His gentle corrections.

He Changed Jesus from a LAMB to a LION
The Lord Jesus went down in death as a gentle and meek

LAMB of God. He was slaughtered for our sin and because He was a LAMB, He did not open His mouth in complaint or hatred; even when they nailed Him to the Cross and pierced His hands, legs and side. **In general, lambs are known to be to very gentle, meek, trusting and submissive; even when you put a knife to a lamb's neck, it does not know to cry out.** The prophet Isaiah prophesied this meekness of God's LAMB in **Isaiah 53:6-8:**

> "All we like sheep have gone astray; we have turned everyone to his own way; and the LORD hath laid on him the iniquity of us all. 7 **He was oppressed, and he was afflicted, yet he opened not his mouth: he is brought as a lamb to the slaughter, and as a sheep before her shearers is dumb, so he openeth not his mouth.** 8 He was taken from prison and from judgment..."

As God's meek and gentle LAMB, the Lord Jesus submitted to His Father's will to go to the Cross and die for us all but on the third day, the **Holy Spirit** who is **the Warrior Side of God** descended into hell and raised Him up back to life as a **Mighty LION:**

> "And I wept much, because no man was found worthy to open and to read the book, neither to look thereon. 5 And one of the elders saith unto me, Weep not: **behold, the Lion of the tribe of Juda**, the Root of David, hath prevailed to open the book, and to loose the seven seals thereof. 6 And I beheld, and, lo, in the midst of the throne and of the four beasts, and in the midst of the elders, **stood a Lamb as it had been slain, having seven horns and seven eyes, which are the seven Spirits of God sent forth into all the earth.**

7 And he came and took the book out of the right hand of him that sat upon the throne. *8* And when he had taken the book, **the four beasts and four and twenty elders fell down before the <u>Lamb</u>**, having every one of them harps, and golden vials full of odours, which are the prayers of saints" (Revelation 5:4-8).

As the **LION of the Tribe of Judah**, He said the following upon His resurrection:

"And Jesus came and spake unto them, saying, **All power is given unto me in heaven and in earth**" (Matthew 28:18).

The Lord Jesus rose up as **the LION of the Tribe of Judah** with power over heaven and earth! **A lion is known to be the only animal in the jungle that runs from no other animal while all the other animals run from it; it is the King of the jungle! It is the lion that pursues, destroys and devours; it is ever the pursuer and never the pursued. This is the basic nature of the lion and it is also known to have the greatest strength in the jungle.** It is why the Lord Jesus is likened to the lion; there is no equal or a match for Him anywhere in heaven, earth and under the earth; only God the Father is greater than Him.

Therefore, when you are talking about the Lord Jesus as the **LION of the Tribe of Judah**, you are really talking about God as the **Man of War** and He wars by the power of the **Holy Spirit**. We need the power of the **Holy Spirit** in our daily warfare but how can we invite Him to help us wage warfare if do not take the time to know Him in depth? Hopefully this book is an eye opener to you when it comes to knowing the Person of the **Holy Spirit**.

He Helped the Lord to Defeat the Devil

The Lord Jesus was able to defeat the devil by the power of the **Holy Spirit** using the **Word of God**. After His baptism, the Lord Jesus was <u>driven </u>into the wilderness by the **Holy Spirit** to be tempted by the devil after His fasting 40 days and forty nights — *"And immediately the Spirit <u>driveth him into the wilderness</u>" (Mark 1:12)*. Also according to **Luke 4:1-8,** the Lord Jesus was <u>**filled with the Holy Spirit**</u> before He went into the wilderness:

> **"And Jesus being full of the <u>Holy Ghost</u> returned from Jordan, and was <u>led *(driven)*</u> by the Spirit into the wilderness**, 2 Being forty days tempted of the devil. And in those days he did eat nothing: and when they were ended, he afterward hungered. 3 And the devil said unto him, If thou be the Son of God, command this stone that it be made bread. 4 And Jesus answered him, saying, **It is written**, <u>That man shall not live by bread alone, but by every word of God</u>.
>
> 5 And the devil, taking him up into an high mountain, shewed unto him all the kingdoms of the world in a moment of time. 6 And the devil said unto him, All this power will I give thee, and the glory of them: for that is delivered unto me; and to whomsoever I will I give it. 7 If thou therefore wilt worship me, all shall be thine. 8 <u>And Jesus answered and said unto him, Get thee behind me, Satan</u>: **for it is written**, <u>Thou shalt worship the Lord thy God, and him only shalt thou serve</u>…"

As you can see, it was the **Holy Spirit** and the **Word of God** that gave Him victory over man's arch enemy — the devil. The **Holy Spirit** empowered Him to confront the devil with the **Word of God** and to boldly rebuke the devil. According to **Nahum 1:2**, <u>God avenges Himself on His enemies</u>; He takes vengeance on His enemies. He needed to save and avenge us from the hand of the devil and He accomplished it all in His Son and by the power of **His Spirit:**

> "God is jealous, and **the LORD revengeth; the LORD revengeth, and is furious; the LORD will take vengeance on his adversaries**, and he reserveth wrath for his enemies."

I remember the day the Lord told me about His plan for the devil by saying, *"I will show him how much he must suffer for what he has done to my children."* I know that God never fails concerning His promises, so I am fully persuaded that He will fully avenge us on the Day of Judgment when He casts the devil and all his demons into the lake of fire. Meanwhile, we that believe are His instruments of punishing the devil on a daily basis because we can rebuke him, bind him and cast him out. We can also recompense his wickedness against us back upon his own head!

Chapter 13
The Holy Spirit is the Finger of God

The **Holy Spirit** is also the **finger of God;** He is the finger that wrote the **Ten Commandments** that were delivered to Moses on two tables of stone. What this means is that God wrote the **Ten Commandments** by **His Spirit** as recorded in **Deuteronomy 9:10:**

> "And the LORD delivered unto me two tables of stone **written with the finger of God;** and on them was written according to all the words, which the LORD spake with you in the mount out of the midst of the fire in the day of the assembly."

In the scripture above, you can clearly see the **Lord Jesus** as the **Word** and the **Holy Spirit** as the **finger of God. God the Father** spoke **the Word** and the **Holy Spirit** —the **Finger** wrote it out.

The Lord Jesus and the Finger of God

Besides coming to save us and to help us put a face to God, the **Lord Jesus** also came to show us God's righteous judgments. He demonstrated the **finger of God** for us and He called the **Lord Holy Spirit** the **finger of God** in **Luke 11:20-22:**

> "**But if I with the finger of God cast out devils, no doubt the kingdom of God is come upon you.** 21 When a strong man armed keepeth his palace, his goods are in peace: 22 But when **a stronger than he** *(speaking of the power of the Holy Spirit)* shall come upon him, and overcome him, he taketh from him all his armour wherein he trusted, and divideth his spoils."

God uses His finger to do the impossible and also to pronounce His righteous judgments. We see **God's finger at work** through the Lord Jesus in **John 8:3-8**. This happened on the day that the Jews brought to Him "a woman caught in adultery." **To me, this incident represents the day that the LAW clashed with GRACE.** The Jews dragged the woman; just the woman and <u>not the man</u> along with her, and they set her before the Lord Jesus in the midst of His teaching session. **They saw the incident as a way to entrap Him concerning obedience to the Law of Moses so; they wanted His opinion about the commandment which states that <u>adulterers are to be stoned to death.</u>**

In their effort to craftily ensnare Him, they informed Him that they caught the woman in "the very act" of adultery and they then added their entrapping question, "<u>but what sayest thou?</u>" **The Lord Jesus must have been amazed at their ignorance of the fact that the same law equally concluded them all to have sinned against God and also worthy of death.** Knowing this, the Lord commanded the first one among them that had no sin to cast the first stone and **He knelt down and He wrote on the ground with His finger** — the finger of God:

> "**And the scribes and Pharisees brought unto him a woman taken in adultery;** and when they had <u>set her in the midst,</u> 4 They say unto him, **Master, this woman was taken in adultery, in the very act.** 5 <u>Now Moses in the law commanded</u> us, that such should be stoned: **but what sayest thou?**
>
> 6 <u>This they said, tempting him, that they might have to accuse him.</u> **But Jesus stooped down, and with his finger wrote on the ground, as though he heard them not.** 7 So when they continued asking him, he lifted up himself, and said unto them, **He that is without sin among you, let him first cast a stone at her.** 8 And **again he stooped down, and wrote on the ground.**"

What do you think the Lord Jesus wrote on the ground? **They <u>may not</u> have been able to read what the Lord wrote**

but they were all aware that the judgment was written <u>in sand</u>; meaning that it cannot be altered or changed. You can conclude the answer to my question by the fact that not one person out of the entire multitude of people dared to cast a stone!

In other words, not one person was willing to risk his or her life and receive the punishment that the Lord <u>wrote in the sand</u>. **The fact that He wrote it twice meant that the judgment was certain.** When **the finger of God writes,** what it writes is a very serious business that cannot be taken lightly. **For example, when it wrote the Ten Commandments, it also wrote the punishment for disobedience — death!**

<u>If anyone had cast a stone that day, the judgment written on the ground by the Lord Jesus would have come upon the person</u>. Knowing the judgment in their hearts, they all began to examine themselves as we see in **John 8:9-11:**

> **"And they which heard it, <u>being convicted by their own conscience</u>, went out one by one, beginning at the eldest, even unto the last: and Jesus was left alone, and the woman standing in the midst.** *10* When Jesus had lifted up himself, and saw none but the woman, he said unto her, Woman, where are those thine accusers? hath no man condemned thee? *11* She said, No man, Lord. And Jesus said unto her, Neither do I condemn thee: go, and sin no more."

Remember that the **Holy Spirit** as the **finger of God** <u>sends and carries out God's Judgments</u>. To fully understand what it means to have the **finger of God** <u>write something</u> or <u>send its judgment</u> against a person, we need to look at what happened to **King Nebuchadnezzar** and his son, **King Belshazzar** in Babylon. The Jews who were trying to entrap the Lord with the woman concerning the law, knew very well what happened in both of these incidents. Their knowledge of God's judgment on King Nebuchadnezzar and his son will also help us to understand why none of them dared to cast a stone at the woman caught in adultery while looking at the Lord Jesus' writing on the ground. Let us see what happened when God sent His Finger (judgment) to King Nebuchadnezzar and his son.

King Nebuchadnezzar and the Finger (Judgment) of God

God used King Nebuchadnezzar to carry out His judgment against the children of Israel because they were disobedient to His commandments. As a result of their disobedience, God decided to let King Nebuchadnezzar carry them away into captivity in Babylon for 70 years. King Nebuchadnezzar was therefore, able to enter Israel, ransack the temple in Jerusalem and take away with him many valuable vessels from the temple. He also took with him the King of Israel and some of the royal children like Daniel and his friends. Because he was God's instrument of judgment against the children of Israel, God also prospered him, his kingdom and his influence grew.

One day, he had a dream of a <u>great image</u> with a "head of gold" and after all his counselors, his wise men, his astrologers, his magicians and his soothsayers failed to give him the interpretation, Daniel who was one of the royal children from Israel interpreted the dream. According to Daniel's interpretation, **God had made King Nebuchadnezzar the "head of gold" (a king of kings) and his kingdom at the time was greater than all the others.** There were other aspects of the dream that I do not need to go into here that you can read for yourself, but the bottom line was that **King Nebuchadnezzar's immediate reaction to being the "head of gold" was to <u>rise up in pride and ascribe all his prosperity and his glory to his own power</u>.** While he was riding high in pride, God sent him His finger — **His judgment** as we can see in **Daniel 4:29-33:**

"At the end of twelve months he walked in the palace of the kingdom of Babylon. *30* <u>The king spake, and said, Is not this great Babylon, that I have built for the house of the kingdom by the might of my power, and for the honour of my majesty?</u> *31* **While the word was in the king's mouth, there fell a voice from heaven, saying, O king Nebuchadnezzar, to thee it is spoken** *(judgment)*; **The kingdom is departed from thee.**

32 **And they shall drive thee from men, and thy dwelling shall be with the beasts of the field: they shall make thee to eat grass as oxen, and seven times** *(7 years)* **shall pass over thee, until thou know that the most High ruleth in the kingdom of men, and giveth it to whomsoever he will.** *33* <u>The same hour was the thing fulfilled upon Nebuchadnezzar</u>: and **he was driven from men, and did eat grass as oxen, and his body was wet with the dew of heaven, till his hairs were grown like eagles' feathers, and his nails like birds' claws."**

Many years later, we again see how the **finger of God** was literally sent to King Nebuchadnezzar's son; King Belshazzar.

King Belshazzar and the Finger of God

There is a popular saying that, **"Those who cannot remember the past are condemned to repeat it."** It turned out to be a true saying in the case of King Belshazzar of Babylon. **He was there when his father, King Nebuchadnezzar experienced firsthand, the horrible consequences of God's finger rising up against someone.** He succeeded his father and became King of Babylon but as you will read, he did not learn from his father's mistakes. He also sinned against God and God judged him as well.

His army also invaded Israel, raided the temple in Jerusalem, took the holy vessels with them and brought them to King Belshazzar in Babylon. These vessels were so highly sanctified that no one but the priests of God were allowed to go near or touch them. **According to the law of purification, the High Priest, Aaron and his children were actually supposed to change their clothes whenever they came out of the Holy of Holies into the outer courts of the temple;** meaning that even the clothes the priests wore into the Holy of Holies were too holy to be touched by those in the outer court. This was to ensure that they do not defile the Holy of Holies and the holy vessels when they return to the Holy of Holies after interacting with the masses in the outer courts. **These holy vessels were now in the possession of King Belshazzar in Babylon.**

Also, it is apparent that King Belshazzar forgot about how God judged his father, King Nebuchadnezzar for his pride and for not honoring the God of Israel. In his state of pride, King Belshazzar made a "great feast" and on this merry making day decided to defile God's holy vessels from the temple in Jerusalem by commanding that they be brought forth into the feast. The Bible says that him and his concubines began to use God's holy vessels to drink and to carry out their lives of debauchery — **Daniel 5:1-4:**

> "Belshazzar the king made a great feast to a thousand of his lords, and drank wine before the thousand. 2 Belshazzar, whiles he tasted the wine, commanded to bring the golden and silver vessels which his father Nebuchadnezzar had taken out of the temple which was in Jerusalem; that the king, and his princes, his wives, and his concubines, might drink therein.
>
> 3 **Then they brought the golden vessels that were taken out of the temple of the house of God which was at Jerusalem; and the king,**

and his princes, his wives, and his concubines, drank in them. 4 <u>They drank wine, and praised the gods of gold, and of silver, of brass, of iron, of wood, and of stone</u>."

While King Belshazzar was carrying on his defilement of God's holy vessels, **God sent His finger to write a judgment against him** as recorded in **Daniel 5:5-6**:

> **"In the same hour came forth <u>fingers of a man's hand</u>, and wrote over against the candlestick upon the plaister of the wall of the king's palace**: **<u>and the king saw the part of the hand that wrote</u>.** 6 Then the king's countenance was changed, and his thoughts troubled him, so that **the joints of his loins were loosed, and his knees smote one against another**."

Upon seeing the finger of God, King Belshazzar began to experience terror and he began to tremble. Below is the judgment that the **finger of God** wrote against King Belshazzar in **Daniel 5:18-31**:

> " *(The reason for the judgment)* O thou king, the most high God gave Nebuchadnezzar thy father a kingdom, and majesty, and glory, and honour: 19 And for the majesty that he gave him, all people, nations, and languages, trembled and feared before him: whom he would he slew; and whom he would he kept alive; and whom he would he set up; and whom he would he put down. 20 But when his heart was lifted up, and his mind hardened in pride, he was deposed from his kingly throne, and they took his glory from him:
>
> 21 <u>And he was driven from the sons of men; and his heart was made like the beasts, and</u>

his dwelling was with the wild asses: they fed him with grass like oxen, and his body was wet with the dew of heaven; till he knew that the most high God ruled in the kingdom of men, and that he appointeth over it whomsoever he will. 22 **And thou his son, O Belshazzar, hast not humbled thine heart, though thou knewest all this;**

23 **But hast lifted up thyself against the Lord of heaven**; and they have **brought the vessels of his house before thee, and thou, and thy lords, thy wives, and thy concubines, have drunk wine in them; and thou hast praised the gods of silver, and gold, of brass, iron, wood, and stone**, which see not, nor hear, nor know: **and the God in whose hand thy breath is, and whose are all thy ways, hast thou not glorified:**

24 Then was **the part of the hand sent from him; and this writing was written.** 25 And this is the writing that was written, **MENE, MENE, TEKEL, UPHARSIN.** 26 This is the interpretation of the thing: MENE; **God hath numbered thy kingdom, and finished it.** 27 TEKEL; **Thou art weighed in the balances, and art found wanting.** 28 PERES; **Thy kingdom is divided, and given to the Medes and Persians**... 30 **In that night was Belshazzar the king of the Chaldeans slain.** 31 And **Darius the Median** took the kingdom, being about threescore and two years old."

As you can see, the judgment immediately came to pass against King Belshazzar of Babylon because he was killed that very night in a coup by **Darius the Median**. It is not a pleasant thing to have **God's finger** write or send a judgment against you.

Chapter 14
The Holy Spirit Reproves the World of Sin

We have seen in some of the previous chapters that the Lord Jesus is the **"Lamb of God that takes away the sin of the world."** In other words, God has done everything that He needed to do in order to purge man's sin but we have to be willing to receive it. **This is where the Holy Spirit comes in to reprove (rebuke for misdeeds) those who reject what God has done for us in Christ.** Why is He going to reprove the world of sin? **The answer is because, when you reject the finished works of Christ, the Bible says that you are <u>calling God a liar</u>.**

He Convicts of Sin and Righteousness

The Bible also tells us that **all creation testifies of God and His works** but a lot of people as well as the <u>atheists</u> do not believe the Bible and they fight against those who do. Their actions do not alter the **truth of God** and of what He did on the Cross for us in Christ. **The Holy Spirit will reprove <u>the world</u> (all unbelievers) of righteousness because we all have been given God's righteousness freely in Christ and the Lord Jesus has gone back to heaven.** You are to receive it gratefully and failure to receive it carries the penalty of eternal damnation in hell.

Therefore, it is the **Holy Spirit** that tells you that the Lord Jesus paid for your sins but if you are saying <u>no</u> to the good news, you are insisting on paying for all your sins by yourself. **Everyone has the inner witness of the Holy Spirit in their conscience and everyone has the capacity to receive Christ but many do not believe or want Him.** For example, He is the one that places a check in your heart when you meet someone with a questionable character; He makes you to be leery of the person. **Because of this inner witness, no one will have the excuse of not knowing about**

the Lord Jesus on Judgment Day. It is the **Lord Holy Spirit** that <u>convicts</u> the world of sin and of the need to receive Christ (righteousness) — **John 16:8-10:**

> "**And when he is come** *(the Holy Spirit)*, **he will** <u>**reprove the world of sin**</u>**, and of righteousness, and of judgment:** 9 **Of sin, because they believe not on me;** 10 **Of righteousness, because I go to my Father, and ye see me no more**…"

The **Lord Jesus** sent us the **Holy Spirit** to make it possible for whoever is willing to receive God's righteousness (new birth) to get it. In other words, anyone who desires it can now get born again by the working of the **Holy Spirit**. <u>This was why the Lord Jesus said that it was expedient that He goes back to heaven so that He can send us the **Holy Spirit**</u>. This is part of the **good news** that we share with the world today — **anyone who is willing can now be born again!** The **Holy Spirit** is here to make it happen.

Knowing this, our prayer for unbelievers is, "Lord, when the Gospel comes to them; please help them to accept it so that they can be born again and receive the **Holy Spirit**" but as you are witnessing to them, you also need the **Holy Spirit** to activate the **Word of God** that you are speaking to them. Some people think that they can use their 'prepared speech' to make someone understand the Word or the ways of God. If you are one of such people, I say to you, forget it because it is the job of the **Holy Spirit**. You cannot do it in your own strength or with your human knowledge.

Our job is to preach the Gospel and it is the job of the **Lord Holy Spirit** to bring the 'conviction' upon the hearts of the people hearing the Gospel. He shows them their need for Christ and how sin has been enslaving them in order for them to desire righteousness. <u>Because God has given us all a free will</u>, we cannot make anyone do anything that they do not want to do; we have to respect their free will. **Therefore, without the Holy Spirit convicting the unbelievers of their sins, talking to them is like talking apples and oranges** and **God the Father once told me that I cannot pick apples from an orange tree.** A lot of times, that is what some people are doing; using their "sense knowledge" to preach the Gospel instead of depending or relying on the **Holy Spirit**.

He Reproves Believers Also

I said before that the **Holy Spirit** is our helper when it comes to carrying out our God-given assignments. He also convicts us when we go outside the will of God. **For example, when you backslide or go back to your old sinful ways after salvation, the Holy Spirit will put a check in your spirit and He will begin to convict you of your wrong doing.** He will also begin to train you by showing you areas in your life that you have to change so that you do not go back to your old ungodly ways. If for instance you defrauded someone, He will at times tell you to go back and repay what you defrauded the person of or He will instruct you to tell the person that you are sorry for defrauding him or her.

He Helps Believers to Enforce the Lord's Victory

The **Lord Jesus** also told us in **John 16:11** that the prince of this world has been judged. Therefore, we should all rise up to kick out the devil in every area of our lives and the lives of our loved ones that he wants to occupy. **He was once the prince of this world but he is now a defeated foe that has already been judged.** He is awaiting his sentence to the lake of fire. **The Lord Jesus is now the Prince of Princes, the King of Kings and the Lord over this world and we are to enforce His victory in our daily lives and everywhere we go:**

> **"Of judgment, because the prince of this world is judged."**

Since the prince of this world has been judged, it is the Holy Spirit that now helps us to rise up against him whenever he comes against us. While we sleep, the Holy Spirit watches over us and rises up against the devil and his evil spirits on our behalf just as long as we do not have active evil covenants with them. This is why we all need to renounce the ungodly covenants that are still active in our lives and in our families because they give the devil legal rights to operate in our lives and they prevent the **Holy Spirit** from intervening to protect or defend us. The **Holy Spirit** helps us to occupy till the Lord Jesus returns:

"**...Occupy till I come**" (Luke 19:13).

Chapter 15
The Holy Spirit Helps Us to Pray God's Will

He Helps Our Weaknesses in Prayer

The **Holy Spirit** helps us to pray God's will and He brings us answers from God because He is a part of God; the very Spirit of God Himself! One of the reasons why some people do not get results when they pray is because they do not incorporate the ministry of the **Holy Spirit** into their prayer lives. I always try to remember the Lord's words in John 15:5 that says, **"For without me ye can do nothing"** and I incorporate it into everything that I do including prayer. After His dealings with me on my early presumptuousness, I never presume to know or be able to do anything on my own without Him and I have seen what His help can accomplish; He does exceedingly far beyond what I can even think of.

Therefore, we all stand to benefit from the scripture in **Romans 8:26-27** that tells us that <u>we do not know what to pray for as we ought</u> and that it is the **Holy Spirit** that helps our <u>weaknesses</u> (infirmities) in this area:

> **"Likewise the Spirit also helpeth our infirmities**: <u>for we know not what we should pray for as we ought</u>: **but the Spirit itself maketh intercession for us with groanings which cannot be uttered.** *27* **And he** *(God)* **that searcheth the hearts knoweth what is the mind of the Spirit, because he maketh intercession for the saints according to the will of God."**

If you notice, the scripture above does not say that <u>we do not know how to pray</u> but that <u>we do not know what we should pray for</u>. Very many of us know how to pray in our prayer closets and do pray on a daily basis; so there is no question about us knowing how to pray. For example, I consider the

'Nigerian Church' (all the born again churches in Nigeria) to be one of the most prayer intense churches there is; the 'Nigerian Church' as a whole is a Prayer Warrior Church. A lot of us can pray for hours just like the 'Nigerian Church' but it is not enough to just pray or to know how to pray; you must know what you are praying for (discernment) and you must see the results of your prayers.

Praying Outside of God's Will

When most Christians are faced with a problem, a lot of them just charge into prayer. In so doing, many pray their own will instead of God's will. If on the other hand in time of trouble they go to the **Holy Spirit**, He will help them to understand what they are dealing with and what to pray in the situation. What am I talking about? I am talking about taking the time to ask the **Lord Holy Spirit** questions about a situation before uttering the first word of prayer about it. I am talking about asking the **Lord Holy Spirit** what to pray concerning what you are dealing with and getting the actual prayer that you are supposed to pray from Him.

It works for me and I advise you to try it the next time something comes up; just ask the **Holy Spirit** what is going on and what to pray concerning it. **When it comes to praying effective prayers, we need the ministering of the Holy Spirit to guide us into the right prayers.** When the **Holy Spirit** gives you what to pray, it produces results rather than you spending your time and energy praying for eight hours and nothing happens.

Praying My Own Will with a Lot of Effort
Many years ago because I was going through so much stuff in my life, I frequently prayed for half a day on a regular basis and I remembered praying for a particular situation for 3 years without an answer. I mean praying on-and-on about it, fasting about it, decreeing about it and

crying before God about it to no avail, until I went home to Nigeria. While at home, my mother's pastor spoke to me about it and I thought his counsel was wrong. When I left the meeting with him, I decided to ask the Lord for His opinion about what the pastor said and to my amazement, He told me that the pastor was right.

Do you know what the pastor said to me that I thought was so wrong and cannot be from God? **He said that I have not asked the Lord about the very thing that I have been praying for and asking the Lord about for 3 years!** *You can imagine my shock when the Lord said that the pastor was right. Therefore, I asked Him what He meant because He and I know that I have been petitioning Him about the matter for years.* **He said to me, yes, I have been praying to Him for 3 years about the matter but that I have been telling Him what I wanted and that "not once" in those 3 years have I asked Him what He wanted me to do in the matter!** *He said, "It has not cross your lips; not even once!"* *I stood frozen and in shock where I was for a long time.*

I discovered that day that it is possible to pray a lot of prayers about something and yet, pray just your will and not transact any business with God in your prayer. My life changed the day that He gave me one of His secrets to walking with Him; **He said to me, "Ask me to teach you how to ask me questions."** *Trust me, you cannot pray wrong when you first ask Him to help you to understand the situation that you are dealing and what to pray about it.*

About My Many Prayers

Again, I pray a lot because I was taught to have a very active prayer life and the Lord gave me the Anointing for intercession. Over the years, I have sent a lot of prayers into heaven and I have prayed prayers that made **God the Father** to command all heaven to hush but there were answers that I needed to see manifest because I was aware that God heard me when I prayed. One day, I called on Him and I invoked the covenant that I have with Him in Christ on the matter. In response He gave me the vision below by the **Holy Spirit.**

Vision

*In this vision, I was with **God the Father** in His classroom in heaven. He let me know that He was holding up His own end of the covenant and that the problem was not on His end. He showed me all the prayers that I have ever prayed and all the prayers I will ever pray in my lifetime. I noticed that He had them all written out on the board in His classroom and that He had prioritized all my prayers; the first on the list was **Knowledge** followed by **Wisdom**, **Understanding**, etc.*

*He came and stood by me and we both reviewed the prayers. I watched as He took a white chalk and walked over to the board leaving me where we were both standing and He checked off my first request which was **Knowledge**. He pointed to the rest of the items on the list as He turned to me saying, "What you need is **knowledge** because **you are yet too ignorant for all these other things that you asked me for.**"*

I am telling you this in order to let you know that we need the **Holy Spirit** to help us understand what to pray for. My prayer request changed because I know that God has heard me and that He is waiting to see some things manifest in my life before He releases what I asked for. He wants to see me manifest the "Fruit of the Spirit" in my life before He releases what He already gave me when I prayed. My experience also reminded me of someone that the Lord had me tell some years ago that He (the Lord) is "not deaf" and that He heard her but that He will not give her what she asked Him for.

I also remember when I was a part of an intercessory team and before I knew better about prayer. In those days, we got together one year to pray and decree somethings that we wanted to see happen and a year later, we were having another prayer month to pray and make decrees again. On the second day, **God the Father** came and stood in the midst with His hands folded across His chest. His question to me then was in essence; don't you all get tired of making the same decrees and wearing yourselves out praying the same prayers year after year? The Lord Jesus also told us the following in **Matthew 6:7-10:**

> **"But when ye pray, <u>use not vain repetitions,</u> as the heathen do: for they think that they shall be heard for their much speaking.** *8* Be not ye therefore like unto them: **for your Father knoweth what things ye have need of, before ye ask him.** *9* After this manner therefore pray ye: Our Father which art in heaven, Hallowed be thy name. *10* Thy kingdom come. Thy **will be done in earth, as it is in heaven."**

Truly, just as I was, many Christians wear themselves out in prayer because they do not know how to seek the **Lord Holy Spirit's** help in prayer. Some fast 21, 30 and 40 days and most times, it is all at their own <u>desire and will</u> and the Lord never instructed them to fast. Even the godly act of fasting can become an act of iniquity (self-will) if not directed by the Lord. Therefore, ask the **Holy Spirit** if you should fast, when to fast and while fasting what you should pray for. **The chosen fast of the Lord is to let the oppressed go free**, to be kind to the fatherless and the widow — **Isaiah 58:5-8:**

> <u>"Is it such a fast that I have chosen? a day for a man to afflict his soul? is it to bow down his head as a bulrush, and to spread sackcloth and ashes under him? wilt thou call this a fast, and an acceptable day to the LORD?</u> *6* **Is not this the**

fast that I have chosen? to loose the bands of wickedness, to undo the heavy burdens, and to let the oppressed go free, and that ye break every yoke?

7 **Is it not to deal thy bread to the hungry, and that thou bring the poor that are cast out to thy house? when thou seest the naked, that thou cover him; and that thou hide not thyself from thine own flesh?** *8* Then shall thy light break forth as the morning, and <u>thine health shall spring forth speedily</u>: and thy righteousness shall go before thee; **the glory of the LORD shall be thy rereward** *(rear guard)*."

As you can see, God has a different fast in mind from us but a lot of us do not want to listen to Him. We think that we can change His heart or move His hand by fasting 21, 30 or 40 days. Fasting is very good so I am not against fasting but what I am saying is that you need to involve the **Holy Spirit** in your prayers and fasting, because <u>He helps us offer the right prayer</u>. When you are praying, listen to what comes up in your spirit because the **Holy Spirit** will stir up a prayer in you if you let Him.

The Prayer of My Spirit

There was another time that the Lord was dealing with me about praying many prayers. <u>Again, He talked about all my prayers that I have prayed and He wanted to let me know that He had taken care of all that concerns me.</u> **He said that while I have been busy offering up numerous prayers, my spirit came before Him and offered up <u>just one prayer</u> on my behalf.** When I heard this, I was very sad because I thought that my spirit had not been praying enough. I wrote about this on page 67 of one of my books titled, ***Unveiling the God-mother.*** Below is an excerpt:

"He then informed me that I had prayed for many different things that I wanted to see or that I wanted to happen in my life. But according to Him, <u>my spirit came before Him and offered just one prayer that covered all that I will ever need in my life</u>. He said, '<u>Your spirit's request is,</u> Keep me as the Apple of your eye; hide me under the shadow of your wings!' He answered my spirit's request."

This prayer by my human spirit was guided by the Holy Spirit. When He told me about this prayer, I began to understand why sometimes I would see myself like a little kid playing at His feet and every once in a while, He would look down to check on me and He would smile. I know now that I am the "Apple of His Eye" and as a result, I am never out of His sight. I have seen Him deal with those who rise up against me and I have seen Him avenge me to the point that now, I just let Him deal with people for me.

This is the God that we serve and I am not the only "Apple of His Eye;" we all are! My Spirit made knowing and living as the "Apple of His Eye" the priority of my relationship with Him and He wanted me to know about it. **Without the help of the Holy Spirit, I could be standing and singing "shandra" for days without targeting my prayers correctly but He guided my spirit to go before God the Father and right into the heart of what we all want from God — to be the "Apple of His Eye!"** As the "Apple of His Eye," you lack for nothing, you are protected, you are provided for, and you prosper in every area of your life. **It is an all-encompassing prayer and God heard it right from the mouth of my spirit and I thank the Lord Holy Spirit for it.**

Chapter 16
Understanding Blasphemy Against the Holy Spirit

Despising the Spirit of Grace

We cannot despise the **Holy Spirit** or His work and we cannot reject what **God the Father** uses Him to do for us in Christ; we are to honor Him. Because the **Holy Spirit** is the grace of God that helps us to accomplish all that God has called us to accomplish, the Apostle Paul warns us in **Hebrews 6:4-6** that those who were once filled with the Holy Spirit and who have tasted the power of God (the Holy Spirit) and then went back into a life of sin are despising the Spirit of grace. **It is impossible for them to recover themselves and return to God through repentance:**

> "**For it is** underline**impossible** **for those who were once enlightened, and have tasted of the heavenly gift, and were made partakers of the Holy Ghost,** 5 **And have tasted the good word of God, and the powers of the world to come,** 6 **If they shall fall away, to renew them again unto repentance;** seeing they crucify to themselves the Son of God afresh, and put him to an open shame."

By going back into sin, they are counting the **Covenant of the blood of the Lord Jesus** that cleansed them from their sins as an unholy thing. Once you are filled with the **Holy Spirit** and you have tasted both the goodness of God and the power of God through Him, you run a risk of being forever lost if you return back to your old sinful ways. This is particularly true of ministers who preach the Gospel to others while secretly living in sin. Many of them would have demonstrated miracles, signs and wonders by the power of the **Holy Spirit** but the Lord said in Matthew 7:23 that He will tell them to get away from Him because He "never knew" them. In other words, He will reject them because they never lived what they preached.

This final outcome is not just for hypocritical preachers but for all those who knew the Word of God and yet lived in iniquities. According to the Apostle Paul in **Hebrews 10:29**, they will all be given the harsher punishment that they deserve on the Day of Judgment:

> "Of how much sorer punishment, suppose ye, shall he be thought worthy, who hath trodden underfoot the Son of God, **and hath counted the blood of the covenant, wherewith he was sanctified, an unholy thing, and hath done despite unto the Spirit of grace?"**

Also, those who reject the Gospel that the **Holy Spirit** helps us to preach to them are equally despising Christ, His works and the **Holy Spirit** because by rejecting the message of salvation, they are calling God a lair as well.

What is Blasphemy Against the Holy Spirit?

To blaspheme God means to say or write something profane or contemptuous about God. We are to be careful not to blaspheme the **Lord Holy Spirit** because He brings us God's grace; meaning that **He is God's instrument of releasing grace to us on earth. Therefore, blaspheming Him leaves one no more avenue to receive God's grace or pardon since the Holy Spirit is the very vehicle through which we receive it. In Matthew 12:31-32, the Lord Jesus told us about the seriousness of committing the <u>unpardonable sin</u>** — blasphemy against the Holy Spirit:

> "Wherefore I say unto you, **All manner of sin and blasphemy shall be forgiven unto men: <u>but the blasphemy against the Holy Ghost shall not be forgiven unto men</u>.** 32 And whosoever speaketh a word against the Son of man, it shall be forgiven him: **but whosoever speaketh against the Holy Ghost, it shall not**

be forgiven him, neither in this world, neither in the world to come."

As you can see from the lips of the **Lord Jesus** Himself, blasphemy against the Holy Spirit is unforgivable. Therefore, those who call the works of the **Holy Spirit** demonic works are committing the unforgiveable sin against the **Holy Spirit**. In other words, reproaching the **Holy Spirit** and His works or ascribing what the Lord did by the power of the **Holy Spirit** to an ungodly source are serious and unforgivable sins from God's perspective.

Why People Are Afraid of Blaspheming the Holy Spirit

The **Holy Spirit** is the gentle side of God and He is the one who uses the blood of the Lord Jesus to procure forgiveness for us from **God the Father**. Therefore, when someone blasphemes the **Holy Spirit**, there is no other avenue for the person to receive God's grace or forgiveness outside of the **Holy Spirit**! This is why the sin against the **Holy Spirit** is instantly damning and many people know it and are afraid. The Lord once gave me an opportunity to see how instantly damning the sin against the **Holy Spirit** is and below is how it happened:

Seven months after my salvation, I had a divine visitation from **God the Father** and He talked to me for hours but before He left, He told me not to tell anyone about the visitation. He left at about 6 am, and by 8 am, I was on the phone with a Christian friend and I narrated to her blow by blow a lot of the things that He told me. **At the end of our conversation, I informed her that God the Father said that I should not say anything to anyone about it but I shared it with her because she was my close friend!**

According to Him, just like Adam I was still very green about the things of God and the importance of obedience to God was not yet part of my list of priorities. Well, little did I know about the major door that my disobedience had opened to the devil to operate against me at the time. On the Friday of the week that **God the Father** visited me, I went to a denominational church that was operating out of a shopping mall in upstate New York.

During the service, I began to see many different things that were wrong with this particular type of service. While there, I saw how the devil can take over a church service and collect the prayers of the members. That day, I also had my first encounter with the spirit of blasphemy and I narrated this encounter in my book titled, **Unveiling the God-Mother, page 87**:

"...Not long after (communion), the priest began to lead the congregation in the Lord's Prayer. Prior to this day and concerning the Lord's Prayer, I had a bad habit of substituting my own words when it got to the place of **'forgive us our trespasses as we forgive those who trespass against us'.** *Instead, I would say,* **'Forgive us our trespasses as we would like others to forgive us our trespasses'.**

As a result of having witnessed how the devil collected the people's prayers into his unclean bowl and because the devil had left, the Lord's Prayer was the only part of the service that I felt I could participate in. When the prayer got to the point where I usually substituted my words, and as soon as I opened my mouth to say my own words, the Lord pulled out a red-hot tong from his burning fire place in heaven and before I knew what hit me, He stamped a white cross right smack in the middle of my tongue! You could smell my flesh burning as my tongue began to sizzle while being branded by the Lord's tong. When He was done, I could not utter my own words as I usually did because my tongue felt dead.

Immediately after He was done branding my tongue, the spirit of <u>obscenity and blasphemy</u> came and tried to jump on my tongue. It began speaking obscenity and blasphemy against God and it began trying to inspire me to speak obscenity and blasphemy against God. It could not stay on my tongue because my tongue was dead to every other word except the Word of God! I did not know how to fight him off but my tongue could not speak what he wanted me to speak. When the spirit could not get my tongue to move, he left. I immediately went on my knees and I thanked the Lord for protecting my tongue from ungodly words."

The Lord's visitation was on a Tuesday and these events took place on the Friday of the same week and by Monday of the following week, I was in a psychiatric hospital! Not long after I came out of the hospital, <u>the evil spirit of blasphemy came back</u> and this time, it was very bold and forceful as he **tried to force feed me words that it wanted me to speak against the Holy Spirit but before it could finish uttering the words against the Holy Spirit, <u>God instantly turned it into a maggot!</u>**

Our God has awesome power and the judgment on those (man or spirit) who speak blasphemy against the **Holy Spirit** is instant and it is irreversible. I thank God that I was also blessed to experience how God protects us who believe in Christ from speaking blasphemy against the **Holy Spirit** even when we are moving in gross ignorance as I was. He sees to it that the devil does not have that power over our tongues as we commit our lives into His hands.

We are all to have a healthy fear of not blaspheming the Lord Holy Spirit but there are people who are living in an ungodly fear of blaspheming the Holy Spirit while others live in constant harassment and accusation by the devil that they have blasphemed the Holy Spirit. The devil uses this harassment on a lot of Christians who are just awakening to the ministry or workings of the **Holy Spirit**. <u>If you are a **born again Christian** and the devil is harassing you with the sin against the **Holy Spirit**, know that you are not alone.</u>

It is a common tactic of his to get you to become discouraged and to give up on your Christian walk. He knows that if he can discourage you by making you believe that you have blasphemed the **Holy Spirit**, he can get you to give up on God. **Even after seeing how God judged the spirit of blasphemy, he used the tactic against me for several years. I was so afraid to say anything or judge any Christian activity; even when I can see clearly that they were wrong because I was terrified of speaking blasphemy against the Holy Spirit.** All that changed when I read that **"we have the mind of Christ"** in **1 Corinthians 2:15-16:**

> **"But he that is spiritual judgeth all things,** yet he himself is judged of no man. *16* <u>For who hath known the mind of the Lord, that he may instruct him?</u> **But we have the mind of Christ."**

There comes a time in our Christian walk when God begins to **"will and do through us according to His good pleasure."** He stirs us up so we can boldly go against ungodliness:

> **"For <u>it is God which worketh in you</u> both <u>to will</u> and <u>to do</u> of his good pleasure"** (Philippians 2:13).

I also learned in **1 John 2:20-21** that because of the **Holy Spirit**, <u>we know all things.</u> It is the **Holy Spirit** that gives us wisdom about life and God's Word:

> **"But ye have an unction from the Holy One, and ye know all things.** *21* I have not written unto you because ye know not the truth, but because ye know it, and that no lie is of the truth."

Once I understood how the Holy Spirit helps me, I began to reject the devil's thoughts that I have committed the <u>unpardonable sin.</u> I refused to let him make me live in the ungodly fear of blaspheming the **Holy Spirit**.

Disobedience to the Holy Spirit vs. Sin Against the Holy Spirit

Can Christians <u>sin against the **Holy Spirit**</u>? The simple answer is **no**, we cannot <u>sin</u> (blaspheme) against the **Holy Spirit** because we are told in **1 John 5:18** that:

> **"We know that whosoever is born of God <u>sinneth not</u>;** but he that is begotten of God keepeth himself, and that wicked one toucheth him not."

The good news is that we who are born again and call Jesus our Lord, <u>cannot blaspheme</u> the **Holy Spirit but on the other hand, many of us have disobeyed the Holy Spirit.** An example of the disobedience of the **Holy Spirit** that we are all guilty of is this. A lot of nights when the **Holy Spirit** wakes us up to pray, we fall back to sleep without obeying Him. **I can safely assume that there is not a single Spirit-filled Christian that is innocent of this.** Now, blaspheming the **Holy Spirit** is a different matter because the Lord Jesus said in **Luke 11:23** that if you are not with Him, you are against Him and we know that we are with Him:

> **"He that is not with me is against me:** and he that gathereth not with me scattereth."

He again said the following in **Matthew 12:25:**

> "And Jesus knew their thoughts, and said unto them, **Every kingdom divided against itself is brought to desolation; and every city or house divided against itself shall not stand."**

Therefore, we cannot be against Him if we are with Him and we do not have to live in the ungodly fear of having blasphemed the **Holy Spirit**. Some people say, *"I think I have blasphemed the **Holy Spirit**"* and my answer is always this, *"If you have blasphemed the **Holy Spirit**, when you walked through the door, I would have seen a giant maggot walking in because those who blaspheme the **Holy Spirit** are turned into instant maggots (an irreversible metamorphosis in the process of decay)."* I also tell them that if they have truly blasphemed the **Holy Spirit**, the devil will be the last person to make them aware of it because he will not want them to seek God concerning it.

The fact that he deems it necessary to inform a person that he or she has blasphemed the **Holy Spirit** means that the person's relationship with the Lord is beginning to grow stronger and more intimate. Now, if a person has truly blasphemed the **Holy Spirit**, that person is 'done for' in the realm of the spirit; his or her sin cannot be forgiven because the person has already metamorphosized into a worm spiritually. **We have to know and assure ourselves that since we are born again (belong to the Lord Jesus), and we call Him our Lord, we are not going to ascribe His works to the devil or speak against the Spirit of Grace.** We should always remember what **1 Corinthians 12:3** says:

> **"Wherefore I give you to understand, that no man speaking by the Spirit of God calleth Jesus accursed** *(speak against)*: and **that no man can say that Jesus is the Lord, but by the Holy Ghost."**

You cannot curse or blaspheme the **Holy Spirit** when you are in Christ; just as you cannot say that Jesus is Lord but by the power of the **Holy Spirit**. **In other words, if you believe that Jesus Christ is Lord, you cannot blaspheme the Holy Spirit because it is by the grace of the Holy Spirit that you say that Jesus is Lord.** The Lord Jesus also said that no man can come to Him "unless my Father draws him" and He draws by His

Spirit — the **Holy Spirit**. We have to live with the confidence that in **Christ Jesus**, we are now one with **God the Father** and the **Lord Holy Spirit**.

Our Attitudes towards the New Move of God

Christians who are actively serving the Lord do not have to be afraid of blaspheming the **Holy Spirit** but <u>they do have to be careful</u> **when they see a new move of God that they do not understand.** Before you put your two cents into a new move and say that it is not of God, go to Him and ask Him about it. I usually stop and ask Him saying, "Father, is this thing of you?" Sometimes He says, "Yes, it is Me; you do not understand it yet." There are times that He says, "No, it is not me."

The reason that I do this is because the Lord told me that when I see something new that is manifesting and that I do not understand, I should always come and ask Him about it. I advise everyone to do the same because according to Him, if we "lean to our own understanding" just because we are older Christians, we can easily become the biggest persecutors of the <u>new move of God</u> because we think we are experts on how He moves. **It is called the Saul syndrome.** Saul thought that he knew all the laws concerning how God operates so, when Christianity came on the scene, he zealously persecuted it. He was in shock for three days when he realized how wrong he was.

Our Wrong Perception of God Concerning Our Sins

Before I stopped all mandated high school church attendance and before my salvation experience, I honestly thought that God marked our attendance every Sunday just as they do at school so, I regarded going to church on Sunday as making sure that I was marked present. Therefore, whenever I showed up for a Sunday service, I would give myself a pat on the back because not only have I done my part to make

Him extend His grace to me for a while, I have also let Him know that heaven was still my choice.

I had a future plan to give Him all my time, attention and to fully serve Him when I got older. As a result, I thought that He was always very pleased whenever I showed up; even if it was once in a blue moon. Did I know what I was supposed to do concerning my relationship with Him? No. Did I really pay attention to much of the sermons on Sundays? No. **I went to church on Sundays just to make sure that whoever was taking attendance in heaven can mark me present <u>but when it came to my sins, I had no doubt then that He was waiting for me so that He can cast me into hell.</u>** To prolong this inevitability, I had a plan to go to the very back of the line on Judgment Day so that I will be one of the very last people to be judged; I figure it might take Him thousands of years to get to me since there are so many people! I also intended to speak my peace before I got sent off.

I developed these ungodly beliefs about God because I read the Islamic Koran before I read the Bible and the first time I tried to read the Bible, I could not go beyond the first few books of the Old Testament. I became angry at God then for commanding Moses and the children of Israel to kill all the people in the land of Canaan that were not Jews. Also, I read that Ishmael; Abraham's first born was driven away because his mother was Egyptian. In my mind at the time, I saw God as being only concerned about the Jews and no one else.

As for the Lord Jesus, I loved Him from day one because He was my friend from the dream; it was His Father that I did know. Not having any relationship with my earthly dad only made matters worse concerning my perception of **God the Father but all that changed when I received the Lord Jesus as my Lord and Savior and the Baptism of the Holy Spirit.** Now, **God the Father** and I have a very, very close relationship on a daily basis and He is the Person of the

Godhead that I see and talk to the most. In the beginning, I saw the Lord Jesus just about every day but He, the Father and I, now have an intimate relationship.

Many people have their own reasons of how and why they developed an ungodly perception about God's willingness to forgive them when they sin. The bottom line is that you need to know the God that you serve very well and intimately so that you can begin to experience His love and enjoy His rest. **You have to rest in the knowledge that God is not out to get you concerning blaspheming the Holy Spirit but that the Holy Spirit has been sent by Him to help you.** In other words, God has <u>not</u> set a trap for us concerning His Spirit but intends for us to have daily fellowship with Him as Our Father through the **Holy Spirit**.

Therefore, if the devil has been lying to you about God's love for you and His willingness to forgive your sins, take a look at the Cross and see the price that the Lord Jesus paid to get you out of hell and into heaven. This is why the Bible says in **John 3:16-17** that God so love us that He gave His only begotten Son to die for us. Trust me, if you and I were the only people on earth, the Lord Jesus would still have come and died for us on the Cross because He is not willing that any of us should perish:

> **"For God so loved the world, that he gave his only begotten Son, that whosoever believeth in him should not perish, but have everlasting life.** 17 For God sent not his Son into the world to condemn the world; but that the world through him might be saved."

And in **2 Peter 3:9** we learn that:

> "The Lord is not slack concerning his promise, as some men count slackness; but is longsuffering

to us-ward, **not willing that any should perish, but that all should come to repentance."**

The Holy Spirit is a Present Help in Danger

The **Holy Spirit** will help you in time of trouble or danger. He is the one that will speak to you when something bad is about to happen and when you listen and follow His instructions, He helps you to avert the danger. Many people have shared their testimonies with me about how they were not aware that an accident was about to happen but when they followed the instruction of the **Holy Spirit** to slow down, change lanes, or not even take a particular route, they avoided the accident. He is here right now and everyday to help and protect us. In my experience, there have been instances that the **Holy Spirit** stepped in to help me in times of danger. Here is one of them:

Some years ago, I went home at the time that they were having an "Eyo; Masquerade Day" in Lagos, Nigeria and I was not aware of it. The original inhabitants of Lagos believed that these masquerades are 'gods' and humans are not to come into contact with them on the streets. Therefore, on the day that these masquerades come out, most people stay off the streets or wait for them to vacate the streets before going out on foot. Some people get in their cars and wind up their car windows because if you wind down your window and the traffic is slow, these masquerades carry whips made of cow hide and they will whip you mercilessly for daring to confront a 'god' on the street in a car with an open window. The men that wear these masquerade masks give themselves over to demons totally and they can take one step from a very far distance and the next thing you know they are right there in front of you with a demonic speed.

Because I now live in the USA, I had forgotten about this evil day in Lagos and on this day, I did not pay attention *to the fact that the street looked deserted. I had a guest and I had walked with the guest to the bus stop but on my way back, I found myself face to face with two of these masquerades. <u>One of them</u> leaped out from nowhere and looked at me with a 'how dare you' type pose.*

*I remember looking at him thinking, oh my God, I do not want these masquerades to mark me up with their whips because they will whip a person and put a permanent mark on the person's face. I have a cousin that was beaten by them years ago on his way back from the hospital and they left him with a permanent mark on his face. Therefore, as soon as he looked at me and was getting ready to charge at me, the **Holy Spirit** rose up inside of me and said, **"If he comes near you, he is a dead man."** <u>I knew it was a sovereign decree from Almighty God so, I stood firm with my hands on my hips</u>! You should have seen it; I stood and said in my heart that I was not moving. He took a look at me for a while and he ran off in the opposite direction. Praise the Lord for His protection.*

Again, <u>both</u> **God the Father** and the **Lord Jesus** are in heaven; everything that we do today with **God the Father** and the **Lord Jesus Christ** is by and through the **Holy Spirit**. We should make Him a part of our daily lives. **Until the dispensation of grace is over and the last person to be born again is, the Holy Spirit remains with us here on earth but when that last person receives the Lord and the <u>last trumpet sounds</u>, both the Holy Spirit and the Church will leave the earth.** This is why we call Him the **Spirit of Grace** because at that time, God's grace will be over for those who did not tap into it while He was here.

Conclusion

Up until now, the **Lord Holy Spirit** is the <u>least understood Person</u> of the **Godhead**. **Hopefully this book has helped me to unveil Him to you by His grace so that you can pursue a more intimate and personal relationship with Him.** He wants you to know Him intimately and He wants to be a part of your daily life. <u>He is the one who will facilitate your relationship with **God the Father** and the **Lord Jesus Christ**</u>.

In order for God to accomplish all of His will in and through you, you need to have a personal relationship with the Lord Jesus (the second Person of the Godhead) as well as a personal relationship with the **Lord Holy Spirit** (the third Person of the Godhead). To do this is very easy; God did not make coming to Him through His Son; the Lord Jesus a complicated process. First, you need to believe and accept the Lord Jesus Christ as your personal Lord and Savior; then you need to ask Him for the baptism of the **Holy Spirit.**

Below is a prayer that will help you to confess your faith in the **Lord Jesus Christ and to invite him into your life as your Lord and Savior**. <u>**Be sure to pray the prayer out loud so that your declaration of faith can be heard in the spiritual realm by God the Father.**</u> Also, you want the devil to hear you reject him.

Confession of Faith in the Lord Jesus Christ:
*"**Lord Jesus**, I believe with all my heart and I confess with my mouth that You are the Son of God and that You came into this world as **God's lamb**. You died on the Cross for my sins and You were buried and on the 3rd day, **God the Father** raised You up again from the dead. Lord Jesus, come into my heart and be my Lord. I repent of all my sins and I ask You to forgive me and wash them away with Your blood.*

*I turn my life over to You so that you can lead and guide me with Your Word. <u>Also, I ask that You baptize me with the **Holy Spirit** to keep me, to teach me the Bible and to help me live my life for Your glory. I choose to forsake all other religions and follow You as the only true way to God</u> (John 14:6); Amen."*

May the Lord bless you abundantly when you pray the above prayer.

— Dr. Mary J. Ogenaarekhua

About the Author

I am a born again Christian who believes in the preservation of human life and the sanctity of marriage as defined by the Bible. I also believe in letting God set our agenda rather than us setting the agenda for Him. Below is the biographical information about me.

Biographical Information

Name: Prophetess Mary J. Ogenaarekhua, PhD (pronounced **Oge-nah-re-qua**).

Founder: Mary J. Ministries, Inc.; To His Glory Publishing Company, Inc.

Educational Background: BA Communications-Journalism, Masters Degree in Public Administration and a PhD in Theology

Dr. Mary Justina Ogenaarekhua was born in Nigeria. She grew up in a Muslim home with her grandparents and she attended Roman Catholic elementary and high schools. The Lord miraculously raised Mary up from the dead when she took a fatal fall in her early years. Prophetess Mary is gifted with the ability to heal the sick, to interpret visions and dreams, to hear the voice of the Lord, to discern spirits and to intercede as a mighty prayer warrior. She is also the Lord's scribe.

Dr. Mary operates in the gift of prophecy with the ability to see into the spiritual realm. God has opened Prophetess Mary's spiritual eyes to see His desire for His people. She's a teacher of the unadulterated Word of God; a true woman of God in rare spiritual form! She holds workshops and conferences as well as teaches and preaches on many topics including **deliverance, healing, visions and dreams, spiritual discernment, understanding the power of covenants, effective prayers, mentoring, leadership training and much more**. She conducts **evangelism and outdoor crusades internationally** with thousands in attendance.

Dr. Mary Justina Ogenaarekhua is the author of the following books:

(1) Unveiling the God-Mother. This book is a biography of *Mary's death and resurrection experience* and her early years in Africa. It details the spiritual events that happened to her before she became a Christian and before she came to the United States. She also discusses some of the events and holidays that a lot of Christians celebrate ignorantly.

(2) Keys to Understanding Your Visions and Dreams: A Classroom Approach. In this book about visions and dreams, she uses the Word of God to instruct the body of Christ on visions and dreams. She applies the first-hand revelation knowledge that she learned from the Lord Himself. This book is a must read for everyone who dreams and everyone who sees visions. It will teach you how to interpret both with the Word of God.

(3) A Teacher's Manual on Visions and Dreams. This manual is designed to teach the average person, bishops, pastors, etc., the basic principles about visions and dreams, about sources of vision and dreams, about identifying the sources of your visions and dreams and about analyzing their contents. It is meant to be used along with the above textbook titled, *Keys to Understanding Your Visions and Dreams*.

(4) How to Discern and Expel Evil Spirits. This is a very powerful book for all those who are called to the healing and deliverance ministry. In it, Dr. Mary answers the questions most people have concerning evil spirits, and she teaches on the origin of evil spirits, how to discern and expel them and she answers the question, "Can a Christian have a demon?" This is a foundational resource for all those who want to walk in great spiritual discernment and to cast out devils.

(5) A Teacher's Manual on Discerning and Expelling Evil Spirits. This is a powerful teacher's tool with a step by step teaching on key principles about evil spirits, the origin of evil spirits and how to identify and expel evil spirits. It is meant to be used along with the above textbook on *How to Discern and Expel Evil Spirits*. If your desire is to teach others, you can follow the teaching strategies outlined in this book.

(6) How I Heard from God: The Power of Personal Prophesy. Prophetess Mary Ogenaarekhua outlines key principles concerning personal prophecy and she lays out a blue print of what to do with your personal prophetic words. She helps the reader understand the conditions that are attached by God to every personal prophetic word. Failure to understand these conditions will keep your God-given prophetic word from coming to pass.

(7) Effective Prayers for Various Situations: Volumes I and II. In *Effective Prayers*, Prophetess Mary outlines principles on how to pray effectively concerning various life situations. Both of these books contain prayers for almost every situation that a lot of Christians battle with. Many have given testimonies about the deliverance and blessings manifested in their lives as a result of praying the prayers in these books.

(8) Keys to Successful Mentoring Relationships. In this book, Dr. Mary outlines the dynamics involved in a mentoring relationship and the actual steps and stages of mentoring. She also highlights the pitfalls to avoid.

(9) A Workbook for Successful Mentoring. This workbook is a powerful teaching guide for all those who want to be mentored and those who desire to mentor others. It is a teacher/

student's valuable tool for teaching and practicing mentoring. It is meant to be used along with the above textbook titled, *Keys to Successful Mentoring Relationships*.

(10) Understanding the Power of Covenants. This book teaches on the power of covenants. Covenants impact our lives for good or for bad on a daily basis. It allows us to learn about how God uses covenants, how the devil uses covenants and how God wants us to use covenants so that we can receive what He has for us and avoid the devil's attempts to use negative covenants to hinder us. Negative covenants can hinder a person's progress throughout the person's life.

(11) Secrets About Writing and Publishing Your Book: What Other Publishers Will Not Tell You. This book is a powerful synopsis of what you need to know in order to write and get your book published and also how to position your book for mass marketing. It is designed to help all those who desire to write and market their books.

(12) The Agenda of the Few. This book is a call for the Church to get back to its God-given purpose for this country (USA); which is to reach all Americans for God. For too long now, the Church has been functioning as though it is only called to one political party –the Republican Party. The issues discussed in this book are meant to remind the reader that there are Ten Commandments in the Bible and that God can choose to address any of these commandments at any given time. Therefore, we must be willing to get the Church out of the Republican Party box that we have placed it in and learn to seek God's will during each presidential election. He is God of the Republicans, the Democrats and the Independents.

(13) The Agenda of the Masses. Just like the *"Agenda of the Few"* above that was written to the Christian Conservatives in the Republican Party, this book addresses what the Lord showed me that a lot of the Christians in the Democratic Party are doing that equally displeases Him. They have allowed a very large segment of the Church to be pulled away by "the agenda of the masses." In other words, they have bought into the ungodly doctrines, ideologies, beliefs, and political views of the masses to the point that now, their version of Christianity within the Democratic Party is essentially "anything goes." In their attempt to please the masses, they have embraced the pagan gods and have lumped their worship together with the worship of the Judeo-Christian God of the Bible.

(14) **What Tribe of Israel Am I From?** This book is designed to answer the questions of some Christians who are trying to determine the tribe of the natural Israel that they are from. The reason they want to know this is because there are some teachings going on in Christendom in which Christians are being assigned to the various tribes of Israel. This book will help anyone to determine the tribe of Israel that they are from. It is an eye-opener for anyone who desires to know the truth.

(15) **Experiencing the Depths of God the Father.** This book is the first in a series of three books titled, *Experiencing the Depths of God the Father, Experiencing the Depths of Jesus Christ,* and *Experiencing the Depths of the Holy Spirit.* It is written to help you know God in depth as well as understand the mysteries that He has coded in His Word for you. Therefore, this book is for you if you want to know God in a deeper way so that you can receive all that He has for you. It is truly a book for all those who want to know God in a deeper more intimate way.

(16) **Experiencing the Depths of Jesus Christ. This book is written to help you know Jesus in depth and to know how He existed in the spiritual realm as well as in the Old Testament before He was manifested as the Son of God on earth.** It is filled with revelation of who the Lord Jesus is and how He has been dealing with us since man fell into sin. You will be excited as you see the Lord Jesus revealed to you in a way that you have never known before.

Dr. Mary O. lives in Atlanta and is the founder of **Mary J. Ministries** and **To His Glory Publishing Company, Inc.** She is an ordained minister with a strong Deliverance Anointing. She has appeared on Trinity Broadcasting Network and other national television programs.

About Mary J. Ministries

Mary J. Ministries was founded by Dr. Mary J. Ogenaarekhua to equip and impart the anointing of God to the Body of Christ, for the purpose of impacting the whole world. Our goal is to help men, women, old and young to build relationships through Bible Studies, Community Outreach, Prayer Support, Caring Ministries, Teaching on Visions and Dreams, Discernment/Deliverance, Evangelism, Mentoring, Fellowship and Special Events.

As an ordained minister, Prophetess Mary O. teaches, trains and activates individuals to properly operate their prophetic gifts, discernment, deliverance and ministry outreach and interpretation of visions and dreams. Teachings provided by Prophetess Mary O. are inspired by God and are balanced biblical principles for the purpose of developing a spirit of excellence, wholeness and GODLY character.

Prophetess Mary O. is committed to helping the Body of Christ and those who do not yet know the Lord Jesus as their personal Savior to understand their God-given purpose. Mary J. Ministries regularly hosts classes, seminars, conferences and crusades in this nation as well as in other countries.

Contact Mary J. Ministries:
Phone: **770-458-7947**
Website: www.maryjministries.org

About To His Glory Publishing Co.

To His Glory Publishing Company, Inc. was also founded by Dr. Mary J. Ogenaarekhua to help writers become published authors. Our goal is to help new and established writers edit, publish and market their work for a reasonable cost.

To His Glory Publishing Company, Inc. offers one of the most cost effective and stress-free ways of getting a manuscript published.

Books published by To His Glory Publishing Company will be made available in most of the major on-line bookstores like Amazon.com, Barnes & Noble.com, Books-a-million. com, etc.

Our authors receive a 40% royalty on the net sales of their books! Upon request, we submit our published books for buyers and distributors such as Wal-Mart, Family Christian Bookstores, drugstores, Publix and Kroger for review and purchase for their chains of stores.

We are a Christian organization with the sole purpose of bringing glory to the name of our Lord Jesus Christ. Therefore, we will not publish obscene or offensive materials.

To His Glory Publishing Company, Inc. reserves the right to reject any manuscript it deems obscene or offensive.

Contact To His Glory Publishing Company, Inc:
Phone: **770-458-7947**
Website: www.tohisglorypublishing.com

Bibliography

Ogenaarekhua, Mary J. *Experiencing the Depths of God the Father.* To His Glory Publishing Company, Lilburn, GA, USA.

Ogenaarekhua, Mary J. *Experiencing the Depths of Jesus Christ.* To His Glory Publishing Company, Lilburn, GA, USA.

Ogenaarekhua, Mary J. *How to Discern and Expel Evil Spirits.* To His Glory Publishing Company, Lilburn, GA, USA.

Ogenaarekhua, Mary J. *Unveiling the God-mother.* To His Glory Publishing Company, Lilburn, GA, USA.

TO HIS GLORY PUBLISHING COMPANY, INC.

463 Dogwood Dr. Lilburn, GA. 30047, U.S.A (770)458-7947

Order Form for Bookstores in the USA

Order Date: _____

Order Placed By: _____   By Fax: _____

Address: _____

_____

City _____ ST/ZIP _____

Phone #: _____

Email: _____

Purchase Order#: _____

Return Policy: Within 1 year but not before 90 Days.

Price	Quantity	List Price
Shipping Method:		
Media:		
UPS:		
FedEx:		
Other (Please Secify):		
Total Price:	Total Quantity:	List Price

Ship To Address: Bill to Address:

To His Glory Publishing

Let Us Publish Your Book

To His Glory Publishing Company will publish your book at the least expensive cost. We pay one of the highest royalties in the industry – 40%! We print on demand and place your book on the major online bookstores such a Amazon.com, Barnesandnoble.com, Bookamillion.com, etc.

Other Books by Prophetess Mary Ogenaarekhua

Understanding the Power of
COVENANTS

Dr. Mary J. Ogenaarekhua

ISBN 978-0-9791566-8-7

ISBN 978-0-9821900-2-9

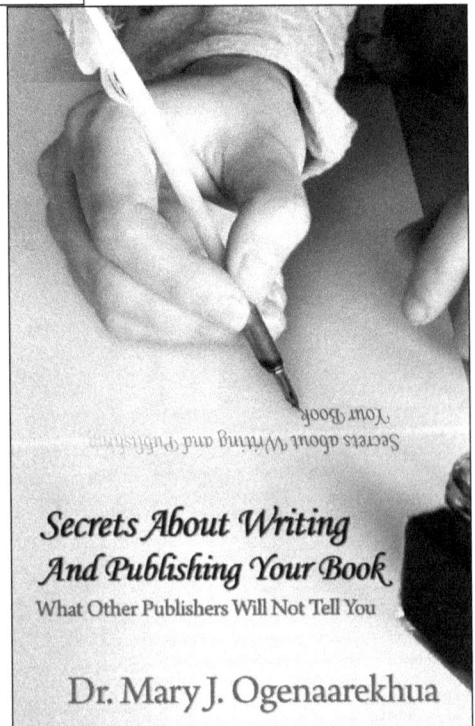

Secrets About Writing and Publishing
Your Book

Secrets About Writing
And Publishing Your Book
What Other Publishers Will Not Tell You

Dr. Mary J. Ogenaarekhua

Other Books by Prophetess Mary Ogenaarekhua

ISBN 978-0-9774265-6-0

ISBN 978-0-9774265-9-1

Other Books by Prophetess Mary Ogenaarekhua

KEYS TO UNDERSTANDING YOUR
VISIONS AND **DREAMS**

A CLASSROOM APPROACH

MARY J. OGENAAREKHUA
AUTHOR OF UNVEILING THE GOD-MOTHER

ISBN 978-0-9749802-1-8

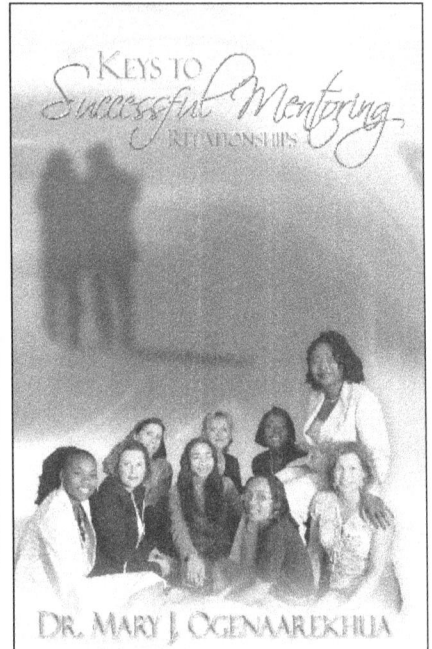

KEYS TO
Successful Mentoring
RELATIONSHIPS

DR. MARY J. OGENAAREKHUA

ISBN 978-0-9791566-6-3

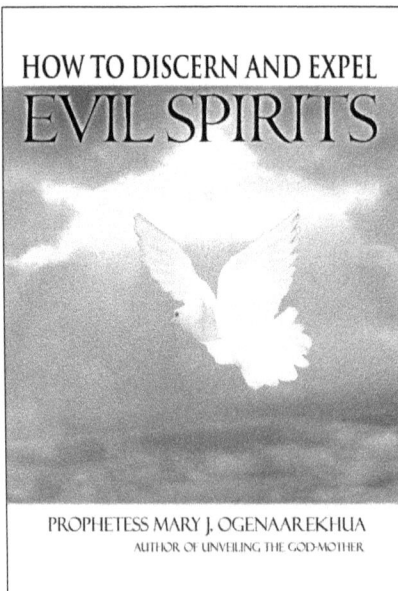

HOW TO DISCERN AND EXPEL
EVIL SPIRITS

PROPHETESS MARY J. OGENAAREKHUA
AUTHOR OF UNVEILING THE GOD-MOTHER

ISBN 978-0-9749802-8-7

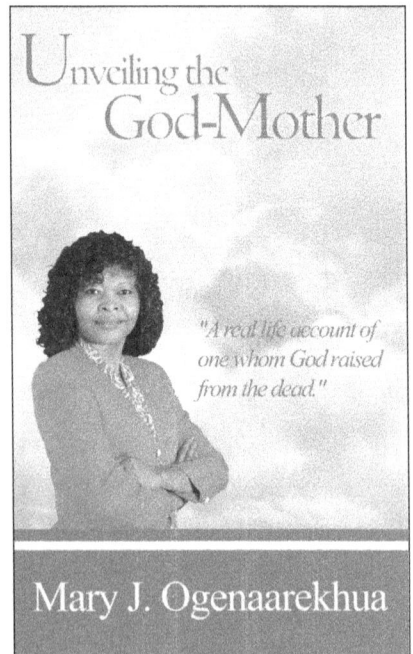

U nveiling the
God-Mother

*"A real life account of
one whom God raised
from the dead."*

Mary J. Ogenaarekhua

ISBN 978-1-5873628-0-4

Other Books by Prophetess Mary Ogenaarekhua

ISBN 978-0-9821900-1-2

ISBN 978-1-5873628-0-4

ISBN 978-0-9821900-4-3

Other Books by Prophetess Mary Ogenaarekhua

ISBN 978-0-9821900-7-4

ISBN 978-0-9821900-8-1